International Labour and Employment Compliance Handbook

www.kluwerlawonline.com

Labour and Employment Compliance in Turkey

International Bar Association

Labour and Employment Compliance in Turkey

Eighth Edition

Elif Nur Çakır Vurgun
Gökhan Akçaalan

This publication is part of the International Labour and Employment Compliance Handbook, available on www.kluwerlawonline.com

Editors: Salvador del Rey and Robert J. Mignin
Associate Editor: Juan Bonilla

INTERNATIONAL BAR ASSOCIATION
the global voice of the legal profession

Wolters Kluwer

Published by:
Kluwer Law International B.V.
PO Box 316
2400 AH Alphen aan den Rijn
The Netherlands
E-mail: lrs-sales@wolterskluwer.com
Website: www.wolterskluwer.com/en/solutions/kluwerlawinternational

Sold and distributed by:
Wolters Kluwer Legal & Regulatory U.S.
7201 McKinney Circle
Frederick, MD 21704
United States of America
E-mail: customer.service@wolterskluwer.com

ISBN 978-94-035-0336-3

e-Book: ISBN 978-94-035-0656-2
web-PDF: ISBN 978-94-035-0666-1

All listed titles are also available on lrus.wolterskluwer.com

1. Argentina: Julio César Stefanoni Zani & Enrique Alfredo Betemps, *Labour and Employment Compliance in Argentina, 10th edition*, 2022 (ISBN 978-94-035-4332-1)
2. Australia: John Tuck, Stephen Price, Rosemary Roach, Jack de Flamingh, Nicholas Ellery & Nick Le Mare, *Labour and Employment Compliance in Australia, 6th edition*, 2021 (ISBN 978-94-035-3914-0)
3. Belgium: Chris Van Olmen, *Labour and Employment Compliance in Belgium, 7th edition*, 2022 (ISBN 978-94-035-4374-1)
4. Brazil: Rodrigo Seizo Takano, Andrea Giamondo Massei & Murilo Caldeira Germiniani, *Labour and Employment Compliance in Brazil, 9th edition*, 2022 (ISBN 978-94-035-4991-0)
5. Canada: Kevin Coon & Adrian Ishak, *Labour and Employment Compliance in Canada, 2nd edition*, 2014 (ISBN 978-90-411-5637-2)
6. Chile: Gerardo Otero A., María Dolores Echeverría F., María de los Ángeles Fernández S. & Javier Sabido, *Labour and Employment Compliance in Chile, 10th edition*, 2022 (ISBN 978-94-035-4404-5)
7. China: King & Wood Mallesons, *Labour and Employment Compliance in China, 6th edition*, 2021 (ISBN 978-94-035-3894-5)
8. France: Pascale Lagesse, *Labour and Employment Compliance in France, 10th edition*, 2022 (ISBN 978-94-035-4384-0)
9. Germany: Gerlind Wisskirchen & Martin Lützeler, *Labour and Employment Compliance in Germany, 10th edition*, 2022 (ISBN 978-94-035-4454-0)
10. India: Manishi Pathak, *Labour and Employment Compliance in India, 10th edition*, 2022 (ISBN 978-94-035-4362-8)
11. Ireland: Duncan Inverarity & Ailbhe Dennehy, *Labour and Employment Compliance in Ireland, 9th edition*, 2022 (ISBN 978-94-035-0326-4)
12. Israel: Pnina Broder-Manor, Helen Raziel & Ilan Winder, *Labour and Employment Compliance in Israel, 9th edition*, 2022 (ISBN 978-94-035-4424-3)
13. Italy: Angelo Zambelli, *Labour and Employment Compliance in Italy, 10th edition*, 2022 (ISBN 978-94-035-4372-7)
14. Japan: Yoshikazu Sugino, *Labour and Employment Compliance in Japan, 10th edition*, 2022 (ISBN 978-94-035-4342-0)
15. Republic of Korea: Sang Wook Cho, Soojung Lee & Christopher Mandel, *Labour and Employment Compliance in the Republic of Korea, 8th edition*, 2022 (ISBN 978-94-035-4434-2)
16. Mexico: Oscar De La Vega Gómez, *Labour and Employment Compliance in Mexico, 10th edition*, 2022 (ISBN 978-94-035-4414-4)
17. The Netherlands: Els de Wind & Cara Pronk, *Labour and Employment Compliance in the Netherlands, 5th edition*, 2022 (ISBN 978-94-035-1594-6)
18. Poland: Barbara Jóźwik, *Labour and Employment Compliance in Poland, 10th edition*, 2022 (ISBN 978-94-035-0316-5)
19. Russia: Anna-Stefaniya Chepik, *Labour and Employment Compliance in Russia*, 2013 (ISBN 978-90-411-4925-1)

20. Saudi Arabia: Sara Khoja & Sarit Thomas, *Labour and Employment Compliance in Saudi Arabia, 5th edition,* 2022 (ISBN 978-94-035-4394-9)
21. South Africa: Susan Stelzner, Stuart Harrison, Brian Patterson & Zahida Ebrahim, *Labour and Employment Compliance in South Africa, 10th edition*, 2022 (ISBN 978-94-035-4474-8)
22. Spain: Salvador del Rey, Ana Campos & Sergi Gálvez Duran, *Labour and Employment Compliance in Spain, 10th edition*, 2022 (978-94-035-4352-9)
23. Turkey: Sertaç Kökenek & Elif Nur Çakır Vurgun, *Labour and Employment Compliance in Turkey, 8th edition*, 2022 (ISBN 978-94-035-0336-3)
24. United Arab Emirates: Sara Khoja & Sarit Thomas, *Labour and Employment Compliance in the United Arab Emirates, 9th edition*, 2022 (ISBN 978-94-035-4444-1)
25. United Kingdom: Ed Mills, Ailie Murray, Anna West, Gareth Walls, Emmie Ellison & Elliot English, *Labour and Employment Compliance in The United Kingdom, 3rd edition*, 2022 (ISBN 978-94-035-4464-9)
26. United States: Andrew J. Boling, Amy de La Lama, William Dugan, Chris Guldberg, Brian Hengesbaugh, Robert J. Mignin, Virginia Mohr, John M. Murphy & Ginger Partee, *Labour and Employment Compliance in the United States, 7th edition*, 2022 (ISBN 978-94-035-3921-8)

International Bar Association
The Global Voice of the Legal Profession

The International Bar Association (IBA), established in 1947, is the world's leading organization of international legal practitioners, bar associations and law societies. The IBA influences the development of international law reform and shapes the future of the legal profession throughout the world. It has a membership of over 40,000 individual lawyers and almost 200 bar associations and law societies spanning all continents. It has considerable expertise in providing assistance to the global legal community.

Grouped into two divisions – the Legal Practice Division and the Public and Professional Interest Division – the IBA covers all practice areas and professional interests, providing members with access to leading experts and up-to-date information. Through the various committees of the divisions, the IBA enables an interchange of information and views among its members as to laws, practices and professional responsibilities relating to the practice of business law around the globe. Additionally, the IBA's high-quality publications and world-class conferences provide unrivalled professional development and network-building opportunities for international legal practitioners and professional associates.

The IBA's Bar Issues Commission provides an invaluable forum for IBA member organisations to discuss all matters relating to law at an international level.

The IBA's Human Rights Institute (IBAHRI) works across the Association, to promote, protect and enforce human rights under a just rule of law, and to preserve the independence of the judiciary and the legal profession worldwide.

Other institutions established by the IBA include the Southern Africa Litigation Centre and the International Legal Assistance Consortium.

Employment and Industrial Relations Law Committee

The aims of the committee are to develop and exchange knowledge of employment and industrial relations law and practice. Members support each other through the provision of innovative ideas and practical assistance on day-to-day issues. In addition, through its journal and through presentations, conferences, the committee ensures the dissemination of up-to-date law and practice in this highly important business area.

International Bar Association Global Employment Institute

The IBA Global Employment Institute (IBA GEI) was formed in early 2010 for the purpose of developing for multinationals and worldwide institutions a global and strategic approach to the key legal issues in the human resources and human capital fields.

Drawing on the resources and expertise of the IBA membership, the IBA GEI will provide a unique contribution in the field of employment, discrimination and immigration law, on a diverse range of global issues, to private and public organizations throughout the world. The IBA GEI is designed to enhance the management, performance and productivity of these organizations and help achieve best practice in their human capital and management functions from a strategic perspective.

The IBA GEI will become the leading voice and authority on global HR issues by virtue of having a number of the world's leading labour and employment practitioners in its ranks, and the support and resource of the world's largest association of international lawyers.

Further information

International Bar Association, 4th Floor, 10 St Bride Street, London EC4A 4AD, United Kingdom, Tel: +44 (0)20 7842 0090, Fax: +44 (0)20 7842 0091, E-mail: member@int-bar.org, www.ibanet.org

About the International Labour and Employment Compliance Handbook

From 1976 through 1988, the International Bar Association and Kluwer Law International published the groundbreaking International Handbook on Contracts of Employment. This Handbook provided one of the first global overviews of the law of the international employment relationship.

Since publishing the first edition, globalization of business has created an increased demand for knowledge of labor and employment laws throughout the world. Therefore, along with Kluwer, we decided to publish an updated Handbook which we have titled the International Labour and Employment Compliance Handbook.

This new Handbook was intended to be a practical guide by providing a general overview of key labor and employment issues in multiple jurisdictions. Each chapter was written so that it is easy to understand by lawyers and non-lawyers alike. Each country author has also followed a standard outline to assist readers in analysing employment issues in each country.

The first edition of this new Handbook included nineteen (19) different countries.

This Handbook would not have been possible without the help and assistance of many people. Most importantly, the individual country authors are all distinguished legal practitioners who spent considerable time drafting and revising their country reports to meet difficult deadlines. We thank each of them. Our friends at Kluwer, especially Ewa Szkatula, have done a wonderful job in keeping the editors and the authors on schedule. Finally, we want to also express our gratitude to Cuatrecasas, Gonçalves Pereira, and Baker & McKenzie LLP for their valuable assistance in the coordination and organization of this project. Our warmest thanks to each of them.

Because of the success of the Handbook, Wolters Kluwer Law & Business decided to publish each country report also as a separate book to give a choice in obtaining the information. We hope this new format will be a helpful and useful resource just like the Handbook. Both formats are available in print and online.

The Editors

Salvador del Rey Guanter
Robert J. Mignin

March 2013

Table of Contents

Authors ix

COVID-19 Information xi

Legal Compliance in Turkey 1

1. Legal Framework: Employment Laws 1

2. Contracts of Employment 2
- 2.1. Overview 2
- 2.2. Written Employment Contracts 4
- 2.3. Oral Contracts 5
- 2.4. Employee Handbooks 5
- 2.5. Job Descriptions 6
- 2.6. Offer Letters 6
- 2.7. Checklist of Dos and Do Nots 6

3. Recruiting, Interviewing, Screening, and Hiring Employees 7
- 3.1. Overview 7
- 3.2. Recruiting 7
- 3.3. Employment Applications 8
- 3.4. Pre-employment Inquiries 9
- 3.5. Pre-employment Tests and Examinations 9
- 3.6. Background, Reference, and Credit Checks 10
- 3.7. Interviewing 13
- 3.8. Hiring Procedures 14
- 3.9. Fines and Penalties 14
- 3.10. Checklist of Dos and Do Nots 16

4. Managing Performance/Conduct 17
- 4.1. Overview 17
- 4.2. Coaching and Counseling 17
- 4.3. Written Evaluations 17

4.4. Warnings and Suspensions 18
4.5. Checklist of Dos and Do Nots 18

5. Termination of Employees for Performance or Disciplinary Reasons 19
5.1. Overview 19
5.1.1. Termination of Employees for Performance 19
5.1.2. Termination of Employees for Disciplinary Reasons 20
5.1.2.1. Termination for Valid Reason 20
5.1.2.2. Termination for a Just Cause 21
5.2. Separation/Severance Pay 23
5.2.1. Termination for Valid Reason 23
5.2.1.1. Notice Compensation *(İhbar Tazminatı)* 23
5.2.1.2. Statutory Seniority Compensation *(Kıdem Tazminatı)* 24
5.2.2. Termination for Just Cause 24
5.3. Fines and Penalties 25
5.4. Checklist of Dos and Do Nots 26

6. Layoffs, Reductions in Force, and/or Redundancies as a Result of Job Eliminations or Other Restructurings 27
6.1. Overview 27
6.2. Reductions in Force/Layoffs/Job Eliminations 27
6.3. Fines and Penalties 29
6.4. Checklist of Dos and Do Nots 29

7. Labor and Employment Law Ramifications upon Acquisition or Sale of a Business 30
7.1. Overview 30
7.2. Acquisition/Merger of a Business 30
7.3. Acquisition Checklist 31
7.4. Sale of a Business 31
7.5. Sale Checklist 32

8. Use of Alternative Workforces: Independent Contractors, Contract Employees, and Temporary or Leased Workers, Telecommuting 32
8.1. Overview 32
8.2. Independent Contractors 32
8.3. Contract Workers 35
8.4. Temporary and Leased Workers, Telecommuting 36
8.5. Checklist of Dos and Do Nots 41

9. Obligation to Bargain Collectively with Trade Unions: Employees' Right to Strike and a Company's Right to Continue Business Operations 41
9.1. Overview of Unions' Right to Organize 41
9.2. Right of Employees to Join Unions 42
9.3. How Employees Select Unions 42
9.4. Pre-election Campaigning 43
9.5. Unfair Labor Practices 44
9.6. Relocation of Work/Shutdown of Business 45
9.7. Checklist of Dos and Do Nots 46

10. Working Conditions: Hours of Work and Payment of Wages by Statute or Collective Agreements 46
10.1. Overview of Wage and Hours Law 46
10.2. Minimum Wage 47
10.3. Overtime 48
10.4. Meal and Rest Periods 49
10.5. Deductions from Salary 49
10.6. Garnishment 49
10.7. Exemptions to Wage and Hours Laws 50
10.8. Child Labor 50
10.9. Recordkeeping Requirements 51
10.9.1. Information That Must Be Maintained 51
10.9.2. Records That Must Be Retained 51
10.9.3. Failure to Maintain Required Records 53
10.10. Reductions in Compensation Caused by Economic Downturn 53
10.11. Checklist of Dos and Do Nots 54

11. Other Working Conditions and Benefits by Statute, Collective Agreements, or Company Policy 54
11.1. Health and Other Insurances 54
11.2. Pension and Retirement Benefits 55
11.3. Vacation and Holiday Payments on Termination 57
11.4. Leaves of Absence 58
11.4.1. Personal Leave 58
11.4.2. Medical or Sick Leave 58
11.4.3. Bereavement Leave 59
11.4.4. Family Leave 59
11.4.5. Pregnancy and Adoption Leave 59
11.4.6. Paternal Leave 61
11.4.7. Injury at Work 61
11.5. Checklist of Dos and Do Nots 62

12. Workers' Compensation 63
12.1. Overview 63
12.2. Checklist of Dos and Do Nots 64

13. Legal Framework for Employee Inventions 65

14. Company's Obligation to Provide Safe and Healthy Workplace 66
14.1. Overview of Safety Regulations 66
14.2. Requirements 66
14.3. Rights of Employees 68
14.4. Rights of Employers 69
14.5. Specific Standards 69
14.6. Injury or Accident at Work 69
14.7. Workplace Violence 70
14.8. Fines and Penalties 70
14.9. Checklist of Dos and Do Nots 71

15. Immigration, Secondment, and Foreign Assignment 72
15.1. Overview of Laws Controlling Immigration 72
15.2. Recruiting, Screening, and Hiring Process 78
15.3. Obligation of Employer to Enforce Immigration Laws 78
15.4. Fines and Penalties 78
15.5. Secondment/Foreign Assignment 79
15.6. Checklist of Dos and Do Nots 79

16. Restrictive Covenants and Protection of Trade Secrets and Confidential Information 80
16.1. Overview 80
16.2. The Law of Trade Secrets 80
16.3. Restrictive Covenants and Non-compete Agreements 80
16.4. Checklist of Dos and Do Nots 81

17. Protection of Whistleblowing Claims 82
17.1. Overview 82
17.2. Checklist of Dos and Do Nots 82

18. Prohibition of Discrimination in the Workplace 82
18.1. Overview of Antidiscrimination Laws 82
18.2. Age Discrimination 83
18.3. Race Discrimination 83
18.4. Sex Discrimination/Sexual Harassment 83
18.5. Handicap and Disability Discrimination 84
18.6. National Origin Discrimination 84

18.7. Religious Discrimination 85
18.8. Military Status Discrimination 85
18.9. Pregnancy Discrimination 85
18.10. Marital Status Discrimination 85
18.11. Sexual Orientation Discrimination 85
18.12. Retaliation 86
18.13. Constructive Discharge 86
18.14. Checklist of Dos and Do Nots 86

19. Smoking in the Workplace 87
19.1. Overview 87
19.2. Checklist of Dos and Do Nots 88

20. Use of Drugs and Alcohol in the Workplace 88
20.1. Overview 88
20.2. Checklist of Dos and Do Nots 88

21. AIDS, HIV, SARS, and Blood-Borne Pathogens 89
21.1. Overview 89
21.2. Checklist of Dos and Do Nots 89

22. Dress and Grooming Requirements 90
22.1. Overview 90
22.2. Checklist of Dos and Do Nots 90

23. Privacy, Technology, and Transfer of Personal Data 90
23.1. Privacy Rights of Employees 90
23.2. Checklist of Dos and Do Nots 92

24. Workplace Investigations for Complaints of Discrimination, Harassment, Fraud, Theft, and Whistleblowing 92
24.1. Overview 92
24.2. Checklist of Dos and Do Nots 92

25. Affirmative Action/Nondiscrimination Requirements 93
25.1. Overview 93
25.2. Checklist of Dos and Do Nots 94

26. Resolution of Labor, Discrimination, and Employment Disputes: Litigation, Arbitration, Mediation, and Conciliation 94
26.1. Internal Dispute Resolution Process 94
26.2. Arbitrary Mediation and Conciliation 95
26.3. Arbitration 96
26.4. Mandatory Mediation and Litigation 97
26.5. Fines, Penalties, and Damages 98
26.6. Checklist of Dos and Do Nots 99

27. Employer Recordkeeping, Data Protection, and Employee Access to Personnel Files and Records 99
27.1. Overview 99
27.2. Personnel Files 99
27.3. Confidentiality Rules 99
27.4. Employee Access 100

28. Required Notices and Postings 100
28.1. Overview 100
28.2. Checklist of Dos and Do Nots 100

Turkey

AUTHORS

Elif Nur Çakır Vurgun

Elif Nur Çakır Vurgun leads the Labor & Employment Practice Group of Esin Attorney Partnership, a member firm of Baker & McKenzie International, a Swiss Verein. She joined Esin Attorney Partnership in 2012.

From November 2013 to May 2014, Ms. Çakır Vurgun was on secondment at Citibank Anonim Şirketi.

Elif Nur Çakır Vurgun's professional memberships include membership in the Istanbul Bar Association (admitted in 2013) and Turkish Bar Association. She graduated from Sankt Georg Austrian High School, Istanbul, in 2008 and thereafter from Bilkent University, Ankara, in 2012.

Ms Çakır Vurgun is fluent in Turkish (native tongue), English, and German.

Ms Çakır Vurgun has authored articles for publication, including the following: co-author, *The Global Employer: Turkey Guide* for 2017, 2018, 2019, 2020 and 2021; co-author, *The Global Employer: Focus on Immigration and Mobility*, Baker & McKenzie, for 2015, 2016, 2017, 2018, 2019, 2020 and 2021 and co-author, Turkey chapter, *International Labour and Employment Compliance Handbook*, Wolters Kluwer, for 2015, 2016, 2017, 2018, 2019, 2020 and 2021.

ADDRESS

Esin Attorney Partnership,
Ebulula Mardin Caddesi, Gül Sokak,
No. 2, Maya Park Tower 2,
Akatlar-Beşiktaş,

Istanbul,
Turkey
Tel.: +90 212 376 64 00
E-mail: elif.cakir@esin.av.tr

Gökhan Akçaalan

Gökhan Akçaalan is a senior associate in the Labor & Employment Practice Group of Esin Attorney Partnership, a member firm of Baker & McKenzie International, a Swiss Verein. He joined Esin Attorney Partnership in 2014. He advises domestic and multinational clients on employment legal matters (individual/collective employment relations), immigration and dispute resolution.

In 2017 and 2018, Gökhan Akçaalan was on secondment at PepsiCo and n11.com.

Gökhan Akçaalan's professional memberships include membership in the Istanbul Bar Association (admitted in 2015) and Turkish Bar Association. He graduated from Yeditepe University, Istanbul, in 2014.

He is fluent in Turkish (native tongue) and English.

He has authored articles for publication, including the following: co-author, *The Global Employer: Turkey Guide for 2019, 2020 and 2021*; co-author, *The Global Employer: Focus on Immigration and Mobility*, Baker & McKenzie, for 2019, 2020 and 2021.

ADDRESS

Esin Attorney Partnership,
Ebulula Mardin Caddesi, Gül Sokak,
No. 2, Maya Park Tower 2,
Akatlar-Beşiktaş,
Istanbul,
Turkey
Tel.: +90 212 376 64 00
E-mail: gokhan.akcaalan@esin.av.tr

COVID-19 Information

Workplace Health and Safety

Employers generally have extensive occupational health and safety obligations. In addition to this, various governmental institutions have issued a number of additional measures to be taken in the workplace in terms of occupational health and safety due to the COVID-19 pandemic. For example, the Ministry of Labor and Social Security (the "*Ministry*") and the Ministry of Health published general and sector-specific guidelines on occupational health and safety measures. Similarly, the Ministry of Industry and Technology issued measures for production centers such as organized industrial zones, factories and technoparks. These guides are available on the relevant ministries' websites.

Occupational health and safety have thus been one of the most controversial issues during the COVID-19 outbreak. In this context, it is imperative that these workplaces have taken the necessary health and safety measures to continue their activities. In fact, it is highly recommended to continue remote working, especially for those who are able to work from home, in order to minimize the risk of the virus spreading in the workplace.

Calling employees back to the workplace may require employers to set company policies or rules on the following topics. It would be useful for employers to discuss these issues with occupational health and safety experts and take the necessary measures before reopening their workplaces:

- maintaining social distance between employees, as well as between employees and visitors and limiting physical contact between these individuals;
- issuing banners and posters about good hygiene practices;
- providing adequate handwashing facilities, hand sanitizer and tissues;
- cleaning communal areas;
- providing employees with information on the symptoms of the virus and what to do if they suspect that they are infected with the virus;

- taking additional measures for employees in the at-risk group;
- isolating the employees showing symptoms or who share a household from individuals showing symptoms and other employees; and
- postponing to the extent possible the business-related travels and meetings.

Besides adhering to the ministerial guidelines and creating new policies and practices, it is essential for employers to train employees on the rules they must comply with.

Although certain measures/restrictions taken due to COVID-19 have been lifted (i.e., curfew rules were lifted as of July 1, 2021) and certain requirements have been bent, as COVID-19 has not yet turned into an endemic from pandemic, employers should continue to apply with any guidance dictated by the government authorities, unless otherwise instructed by the government authorities.

Notifications Requirements for Suspected and Confirmed Cases

The employer must immediately notify an authorized healthcare organization affiliated with the Ministry of Health if an employee or other worker working at an employer's site is suspected and/or confirmed with COVID-19.

There were uncertainties as to whether COVID-19 would be considered an occupational accident or occupational disease. The Social Security Institution clarified the issue with the circular dated May 7, 2020. COVID-19 was accepted as an illness and not as an occupational accident or occupational disease. In this regard, employers are not required to report COVID-19 cases among their employees to the Social Security Institution as occupational accidents or occupational diseases. COVID-19-positive employees must, however, be treated as "sick employees," i.e., be notified as temporarily disabled (*geçici iş göremezlik*) to the Social Security Institution.

Even if COVID-19 is accepted as an illness and not as an occupational accident or occupational disease by the Social Security Institution, COVID-19-positive employees can file lawsuits and request from the court that their illnesses are accepted as an occupational accident or occupational disease. In this case, employers must handle the situation carefully and make sure to comply with all health and security obligations, including notifying the respective governmental authorities. Taking the necessary health and safety measures explained above can reduce the spread of the virus and therefore the number of cases, as well as reduce or eliminate the employer's liability.

If the illness is accepted as an occupational accident or occupational disease, depending on the employer's liability, the employee may demand compensation for the pecuniary and non-pecuniary damages they suffer due to an occupational accident. If the employee has died as a result of the accident, the employee's legal heirs may also demand compensation for pecuniary and non-pecuniary damages. Furthermore, the employee's heirs may demand compensation for loss of support.

Legal Compliance in Turkey

1. LEGAL FRAMEWORK: EMPLOYMENT LAWS

The Constitution of the Republic of Turkey (the "Turkish Constitution") is at the top of the hierarchy of Turkish norms and thus any law that is contrary to the Turkish Constitution is invalid. Article 49 of the Turkish Constitution ascertains that everyone has the right and responsibility to work.

Employment relationships are governed by the Labor Code, which entered into force on June 10, 2003. The Turkish Code of Obligations No. 6098 (the "Code of Obligations"), ratified on July 1, 2012, modernizes the former Code of Obligations and supplements the Labor Code's provisions on employment relationships. The Code of Obligations introduced provisions on releases, bonuses, non-compete, and general terms and conditions.

The Labor Code oversees most employment relationships, and in instances where it does not offer provisions for particular relationships, the Code of Obligations is applicable. Certain employment relationships are governed under other laws, such as the Maritime Labor Code No. 854 and the Press Labor Code No. 5953, which are *lex specialis*.

International treaties that are in effect possess the force of law, according to Article 90 of the Turkish Constitution. These treaties, however, cannot be appealed. Should an international treaty and Turkish law have conflicting provisions about the same issue on fundamental rights and freedoms, the international treaty trumps Turkish law. Turkey is a Member State of the International Labor Organization (ILO) and thus is bound to ILO's standards and rules.

The hierarchy of norms in the Turkish legal order is laws, decrees of the President of the Republic (*cumhurbaşkanlığı kararnameleri*), regulations (*yönetmelik*) and communiqués (*tebliğ*).

Legal doctrine and court precedents are additional wellsprings of employment laws. The Turkish Supreme Court of Appeals (the "Supreme

Court of Appeals") decisions are vital in interpreting the law and clarifying legal uncertainties.

Turkish employment laws also stem from individual employment contracts, collective bargaining contracts, employer guidelines, and workplace practices and regulations.

2. CONTRACTS OF EMPLOYMENT

2.1. Overview

There are two types of duration-specific employment contracts under the Labor Code: (i) indefinite-term employment contracts and (ii) definite-term employment contracts.

The Labor Code primarily recognizes indefinite-term employment contracts, which grant employees the right to seek employment reinstatement.

Definite-term contracts must be made in writing and be executed based on the existence of an objective reason, such as the completion of a particular work, the performance of a particular temporary assignment. If a definite-term employment contract does not rely on such objective reason, the contract is considered an indefinite-term employment contract, no matter what the parties have expressly agreed to otherwise. Existence of such objective reason is also required for the renewal of a definite-term employment contract. Definite-term contracts that do not set forth objective reasons cannot be renewed, and the definite-term employment contract is deemed an indefinite-term employment contract from the beginning.

In part-time employment relationships, which are defined as employment in which an employee's regular weekly work time is substantially less or shorter than a full-time employee's (less than two-thirds of a full-time employee's regular weekly work time; for example, if the total weekly working hours of the full-time workers are forty-five hours, the total weekly working hours of the part-time employees cannot exceed thirty hours), employees enjoy the same monetary rights and benefits of full-time employees, but on a pro-rated basis.

A probationary period can be included in employment contracts. The probationary period permits both the employer and the employee to terminate the contract during the period without providing a notice period or paying compensation. An employee's right to receive salaries and other receivables is reserved, as the probationary period is considered part of their service. In a standard contract, the maximum probationary period is two months; in a collective bargaining contract, the maximum is four months.

Article 20 of the Code of Obligations defines general terms and conditions as "contractual provisions prepared in advance and presented to the counterparty by the drafter of a contract for the purpose of using the same draft to conclude multiple similar contracts in the future." In a contract, the drafting party must inform the counterparty of their general terms and conditions, allow them sufficient time to review the scope of the terms, and receive the counterparty's approval. Otherwise, the general terms and conditions become null. The drafting party cannot draft or enforce provisions that allow them to create unilateral amendments to a contract, including general terms and conditions, which would be to the counterparty's detriment. Among others, employers must therefore take into account the Code of Obligations' provisions while drafting employment contracts.

Certain restrictions govern employment contracts:

(a) Age:

(i) In principle, it is illegal to employ children who have not yet completed the full age of 15. However, children who have completed the full age of 14 and completed their primary education can be employed to do light work that does not threaten their physical, mental, social, and moral development. Children who are continuing their education cannot have their school attendance disrupted because of their employment. Children who have not completed the full age of 14, if their employment does not threaten their physical, mental, social, and moral development, and those under the specified age and who continue their education, provided that their employment does not disrupt their school attendance, can be employed in art, culture and advertisement-related activities. These types of employment require separate written agreements for each activity.

(ii) Men under 18 years old cannot be employed in underground or underwater work, such as mining, cable laying, and sewer and tunnel construction.

(iii) Children and young employees under 18 years old cannot perform industrial work in the nighttime.

(b) Gender:

(i) Women of any age cannot be employed in underground or underwater work, such as mining, cable laying, and sewer and tunnel construction.

(c) Health Conditions:

(i) Children and young employees can only perform certain jobs determined by the relevant regulation.

   (ii) Individuals working in “hazardous” and “highly hazardous” workplaces must obtain a health report indicative of their physical and mental suitability prior to beginning employment.

(d) Foreign Nationals:

   (i) In principle, foreign nationals can be employed in Turkey only if they obtain a work permit. Foreign nationals are not able to carry out some jobs (public notary, attorney etc.) which are indigenous to Turkish citizens.

2.2. Written Employment Contracts

There is no specific format for general employment contracts under the Labor Code or the Code of Obligations, unless otherwise indicated in the Labor Code.

Definite-term employment contracts, telecommuting (i.e., remote working) contracts, and on-call-work employment contracts (*çağrı üzerine çalışma*), must be executed in writing but not in any specific format. For other employment contracts that do not need to be executed in writing, the employer must provide the employee with a written document delineating the general and specific terms and conditions of work within two months from the employee’s start date of employment. The general and specific terms and conditions of work document (the “work conditions document”) include the daily and weekly work hours, duration of a definite-term contract, base salary and benefits, pay disbursement schedule, and conditions for contract termination. If the contract terminates before the completion of the two-month period, the employer must deliver the work conditions document to the employee on the termination date at the latest. Employers who do not provide their employees with work conditions documents will face an administrative fine. The penalty amount varies each year.

The relevant authorities require the submission of written employment contracts prior to processing work permit applications. Therefore, in practice, the written form for employment contracts may become an obligation even if the law does not require the conclusion of a written contract.

Written contracts are an essential piece of evidence. In court disputes, a written employment contract executed between the parties is a boon in demonstrating, for instance, the pay disbursement schedule, the employee’s benefits, notice periods, or post-employment conditions.

2.3. Oral Contracts

An oral employment contract is valid and binding on both parties since, as noted in section 2.2., there is no specific format for general employment contracts.

2.4. Employee Handbooks

In Turkey, employee handbooks are generally used to communicate "workplace rules." Multinational companies or more regimented workplaces like banks, with human resources departments, primarily utilize workplace regulations.

Article 22 of the Labor Code states that workplace regulations are part of the employment contract. Workplace regulations must comply with statutory requirements, and the employee accepts them as part of their employment contract.

The employer is not required to have the workplace regulations reviewed by governmental authorities prior to their issuance. Workplace regulations, however, may qualify as general terms and conditions (*see* section 2.1.), as they are prepared in advance, utilized to execute various and similar future regulations, and presented to employees for review and acceptance.

Workplace regulations are only valid if the employee is clearly informed about and accepts the regulations when concluding the employment contract. In this regard, for instance, displaying workplace regulations on a bulletin board in the workplace's common areas is not a sufficient or appropriate way to clearly inform employees of the workplace regulations. The appropriate course of action is to: (i) provide the employee with a copy of the workplace regulations; (ii) explain the regulations to the employee; (iii) allow the employee time to review the regulations; and (iv) procure a copy of the regulations wet signed by the employee and preserve it in the employee's personnel file.

The employer can make significant adverse changes to the working conditions indicated in the employment contract or workplace regulations/practices only with the employee's prior written consent. Significant adverse changes include adverse alterations to salary and monetary benefits, responsibilities/job description, workplace, and working hours. The employer must inform the employee of the proposed changes in writing and receive the employee's written consent. Changes enacted without following such procedure, and that the employee does not accept in writing within six business days following receipt of the written proposed changes, are not binding on the employee.

If the employee does not accept the proposed changes within six business days following the receipt of the written proposed changes, the employer can terminate the contract if it has a valid reason or just cause. The employee's refusal to accept the proposed change is not merely a valid reason for termination.

Should the employer insist on undertaking the proposed changes despite the employee's refusal, the employee has the right to terminate employment based on just cause. Termination based on just cause, in such case, leads to a constructive termination wherein the employee can terminate employment immediately and demand statutory seniority compensation.

2.5. Job Descriptions

In principle, employment contracts determine the employee's responsibilities, functions, and tasks. The employer's right to issue additional directives is limited to tasks that comply with, are similar to, and have an equivalent value to the employee's work. Job descriptions should be as clear as possible to make the employee understand the scope of their tasks and the employer's expectations but also should enable the employer to enlarge the work's scope.

Being directed to do work differently from the work indicated in their employment contract or forced to work in less than favorable conditions are significant adverse changes to the employee's working conditions. Consult section 2.4. for elaborations on the requirement to obtain the employee's written consent to any significant adverse changes and the employer and employee's rights of termination arising from significant adverse changes.

2.6. Offer Letters

It is possible for employers to issue offer letters to their job candidates. Offer letters must clearly establish whether the employer is issuing a binding or nonbinding offer through their delivery. In particular, if the offer letter will not be binding or is subject to certain conditions, this must be expressly stated in the letter.

2.7. Checklist of Dos and Do Nots

- Execute and sign written employment contracts with employees and preserve an original signed copy in each employee's personnel file.

- Carefully review the conditions and renewals of definite-term employment contracts.
- Comply with employment contract restrictions regarding age, gender, health conditions, and nationality.
- Inform employees about, and ensure their comprehension of the terms and conditions in employment contracts, employment handbooks, and workplace regulations that might be considered general terms and conditions. Allow the employee to have sufficient time to review these documents. Obtain and preserve a copy of the documents wet-signed by the employees in each employee's personnel file.
- Obtain employees' written consent within six business days following receipt of the written proposed changes prior to enacting any changes in their salary, work (i.e., job description), workplace, or working hours that may be to their detriment.

3. RECRUITING, INTERVIEWING, SCREENING, AND HIRING EMPLOYEES

3.1. Overview

In seeking the best-qualified employee for the job, it is essential to screen and interview candidates meticulously.

3.2. Recruiting

Employers utilize a variety of mediums to recruit candidates in Turkey, such as job postings, electronic bulletin boards on employers' websites, employment websites (https://www.kariyer.net/, www.secretcv.com, www.yenibiris.com, etc.), social media platforms (LinkedIn etc.), newspaper advertisements, headhunting agencies, and the Turkish Employment Agency.

Article 5 of the Labor Code decrees that, save for reasons related to biological differences between males and females or the nature of the work, an employer cannot discriminate, directly or indirectly, against an employee due to gender or pregnancy during the conclusion, implementation, or termination of their employment contract. An employer cannot pay an employee doing the same or similar work as an employee of the opposite sex a lower salary because of their gender. The Law on Turkish Institution of Human Rights and Equality No. 6701 (the "Law on the Turkish Institution of Human Rights and Equality") reinforces Article 5 of the Labor Code, prohibiting an employer or their authorized representative from rejecting a candidate due to pregnancy, maternity, or the fact that the employee has to take care of their child.

Article 25 of the Law on Unions and Collective Bargaining Contracts No. 6356 (the "Unions Law") states that employees cannot be hired based on whether they are a union or nonunion member, continue to be a union member, withdraw their union membership, become a union member, or do not become a union member.

Employers cannot discriminate against employees with disabilities in any aspect of employment, such as applications, recruitment, working hours and working conditions, as per Article 14 of the Law on Disabled People No. 5378.

The Law on the Turkish Institution of Human Rights and Equality expressly prohibits employers or their authorized representatives from discriminating against:

- employees;
- candidates;
- those who are in the workplace to gain practical experience or who apply to the employer for this purpose;
- individuals requesting information about the work or workplace, to work as an employee or gain practical experience;

in respect of any work-related process for the individuals mentioned above, including the individuals' information requests, applications, selection criteria, hiring criteria, employment, and termination. This applies to job postings, workplaces, working conditions, access to all levels and types of vocational guidance, vocational training and retraining, promotion and being promoted to all levels of employment, on-the-job training, additional benefits, and similar issues.

The above is applicable to all employment agreements, whether or not they are under the scope of the Labor Code.

Job postings should, therefore, not be gender, union, and disability inclusive but should refrain from discriminating against candidates in any manner or form.

3.3. Employment Applications

Taking into consideration the guidelines detailed in section 3.2., employment applications should not request information on gender, pregnancy, maternity, union membership, or disabilities.

Candidates generally submit their CVs, a cover letter, photograph, and references electronically.

Candidates should inform employers of any factors making them unsuitable or unqualified for the position they are applying for. If an employee misleads the employer by falsely claiming to possess certain qualifications or meet certain conditions indispensable to the position, providing false information, or making false statements, the employer is entitled to terminate the employment immediately, pursuant to Article 25 of the Labor Code. Immediate terminations based on false information furnished by the employee constitute just cause and do not require the employer to pay the employee statutory seniority compensation.

Employers should carefully review the candidate's application documents to discern whether the candidate possesses the appropriate qualifications and meets the necessary requirements.

Also, employers should be careful to avoid committing any kind of discrimination while vetting candidates or sharing the candidates' information with any third parties.

3.4. Pre-employment Inquiries

On occasion, the information a candidate provides may not be sufficient for the employer to decide whether to hire them. Employers can request additional information from the candidates, if they are relevant to the recruitment process and the position discussed. Employees should answer these follow-up questions honestly.

As discussed in section 3.3., candidates should inform employers of any factors that make them unsuitable or unqualified for the position. Breaching this obligation allows the employer to terminate the contract based on just cause.

It is argued that employees should have the right to refrain from answering any employer questions regarding gender, pregnancy, maternity, disability, or union membership, as employers are prohibited from discriminating against employees due to any of such conditions.

3.5. Pre-employment Tests and Examinations

Employees are required to undergo physical health examinations prior to beginning employment, pursuant to the Occupational Health and Safety Law No. 6331 (the "Occupational Health and Safety Law"). A report detailing whether the employees' health is adequate for their workplace duties must be obtained from the workplace doctor by the employer for each employee. For workplaces with less than fifty employees and which are classified as "less hazardous," such report can be obtained from public service providers or family doctors.

For workplaces classified as "hazardous" or "highly hazardous," a health report for the employee prior to their start date, stating that the employee fits for the work, must be obtained.

Employers who breach the physical health report requirement will face an administrative fine for each employee lacking a health report. The penalty amount varies each year.

3.6. Background, Reference, and Credit Checks

Employers in Turkey commonly request supplementary information from their employees, such as work history, personal references, and criminal records. Employers can also request the employee's credit score and history, though this practice is uncommon in Turkey. However, the employer does not have unlimited access to their employee's personal data.

Article 20 of the Turkish Constitution:

> Everyone has the right to request the protection of their personal data. This right includes being informed of, having access to and requesting the correction or deletion of their personal data, and to find out whether these are used in line with their objectives. Personal data can be processed only in cases set forth in the law or upon the person's explicit consent. The principles and procedures regarding the protection of personal data shall be regulated by law.

Law No. 6698 on the Protection of Personal Data (the "Data Protection Law") entered into force on April 7, 2016.

The Data Protection Law defines personal data as "any information relating to an identified or identifiable real person," whereas special categories of personal data ("sensitive personal data") are defined as "personal data relating to the race, ethnicity, political opinion, philosophical belief, religion, sect or other beliefs, appearance and clothes, membership to an association, foundation or union, health, sexual life, criminal conviction and security measures as well as biometrical and genetic data."

Processing is defined as "any operation which is performed upon personal data, whether by automatic means or non-automatic means on the condition that it is a part of any data filing system, such as collection, recording, storage, conservation, modification, rearrangement, disclosure, transmission, taking over, making available, classification or blocking of use" under the Data Protection Law.

The Data Protection Law defines the term "data controller" as "the natural or legal person who determines the purposes and means of processing personal data and who is responsible for the establishment and management of a data filing system." Accordingly, employers qualify as data controllers within the scope of processing employees' personal data.

When processing employee data, employers must comply with certain principles set forth by the Data Protection Law:

- Data processing must be in accordance with the law and the principle of good faith.
- Data processed must be accurate and up-to-date.
- Data must be processed for specific, clear, and legitimate purposes.
- Data processing must be limited and proportional to the purposes for which it is processed.
- Data must be retained only for the period prescribed by the law or necessary for processing.

Under the Data Protection Law, employers must rely on one of the following processing conditions:

- explicit consent of the employee;
- processing is permitted by law;
- processing is necessary to protect the vital interests of third parties;
- processing is necessary to protect the vital interests of data subjects whose consent cannot be obtained due to physical impossibilities or whose consent would not normally be valid and binding;
- processing is in respect to parties to a contract, so long as the data is directly related to the formation or performance of the contract;
- processing is necessary for complying with a legal obligation to which the data controller is subject;
- processing is necessary for the establishment, performance, or protection of a right; or
- processing is mandatory for the data controller's legitimate interest, so long as it does not harm the data subject's fundamental rights or freedoms.

That said, the Data Protection Law provides a more restrictive regime for the processing of sensitive personal data. As a rule, these data may be processed only if employee's explicit consent exists. Unlike non-sensitive data, the only exception to the requirement to obtain consent is where the processing is specifically permitted by law, but this exception does not apply to data relating to health condition or sexual life. To process data related to health condition or sexual life without consent, the data must be processed by those who are under a confidentiality obligation and only for the purposes of protecting public health, preventative medicine, medical diagnosis, medical treatment and care, or for planning, managing, or financing health services.

There is no guidance as to whether employees' consent would satisfy the explicit consent criteria under the Data Protection Law. More specifically, it may be doubtful in many cases that employees would "freely" give their consent to their employers. Therefore, for the processing of personal data, it would be recommended for employers to rely on one of the legal bases of processing personal data listed above other than explicit consent for processing employees' personal data. In jurisdictions with similar laws, two of the most used legal bases for processing data in the absence of explicit consent are:

(1) processing personal data for the fulfillment or execution of the employment contract, and
(2) processing personal data for legitimate interests of the employer.

For example, monitoring employees or conducting performance reviews for employees may generally fall under the second case above. That said, these legal bases are interpreted in a narrow manner, and a case-by-case analysis is required to identify whether the employer can rely on these legal bases.

Moreover, for the processing of sensitive data, employers may not be able to rely on the explicit consent of employees for such processing. In such case, processing sensitive data of employees may be problematic since the exceptions to process data in the absence of explicit consent are limited. That said, considering that obtaining criminal records from employees is a common practice among employers in Turkey. The risks associated with such processing would not be high for the time being.

Employers must, either ex officio or upon their employees' requests, delete, destruct, or anonymize personal data if there is no further need for data processing, even when the personal data was processed in line with the Data Protection Law and other relevant laws. Failure to comply with this obligation constitutes a crime under the Turkish Criminal Code No. 5237, the penalties of which are discussed in section 3.9.

When collecting and processing personal data, employers qualify as data controllers. As data controllers, employers must inform employees regarding certain key issues associated with data processing prior to collection of personal data (e.g., through a privacy notice):

- the employer's, i.e., the data controller's, identity and their representative, if any;
- the purpose of data processing;
- the third parties to whom personal data can be transferred (in Turkey or abroad) and the purpose of such transfer;
- the methods and legal grounds of data collection; and
- the employees' rights (elaborated below).

Employers must take and maintain all appropriate necessary technical and administrative measures to:

– prevent illegal processing of personal data;
– prevent illegal access to personal data; and
– ensure security of personal data.

Employees, as data subjects, have the following rights regarding the processing of their personal data under Article 11 of the Data Protection Law:

(a) to learn whether their personal data is being processed;
(b) if it is processed, to request information with regard to processing;
(c) to learn purposes of the processing and whether they are used for such purpose or not;
(d) to know the third persons within or outside the country to whom the personal data are transferred;
(e) to request correction of the personal data if the data is processed incompletely or inaccurately;
(f) to request deletion or destruction of the personal data under the conditions set forth in Article 7 of the Data Protection Law;
(g) to request notifying third persons to whom the personal data are transferred, about the processes completed within the scope of (e) and (f);
(h) to object to negative consequences about the relevant employee that are concluded as a result of analysis of the processed personal data exclusively by automatic means; and
(i) to claim indemnification if the employee suffered damage due to illegal processing of their personal data.

Article 75 of the Labor Code states that the employer must utilize the employee data obtained under the principle of good faith and in line with the relevant laws and ensure the confidentiality of the data, should the employee have a justified interest in keeping the data confidential.

Article 419 of the Code of Obligations supplements these notions by stating that the employer can only utilize the employee's personal data to ascertain if the employee is suitable for their position or where it is necessary for the performance of the work.

3.7. Interviewing

Employers are bound by certain restrictions to prevent them from discriminating against candidates during the recruitment process, as discussed in section 3.2. Considering the Law on the Turkish Institution of

Human Rights and Equality, employers should conduct the interview process according to the same guidelines against discrimination they follow during recruitment.

During the interview process, employers should avoid discriminatory questions in general, and specifically discriminatory questions about gender, pregnancy, maternity, disability, or union membership. Employers should note that any information on the foregoing categories might constitute sensitive personal data and be subject to strict requirements, as explained above.

3.8. Hiring Procedures

Employers should abide by the hiring restrictions listed in section 3.2. On the other hand, the employer has the right to base their hiring decision on the candidate's education, professional experience, skills, and any other position-related factors provided that the employer does not base their decision on any discriminatory criteria.

Employers must substantiate their decision to not hire a candidate to avoid the fines and penalties discussed in section 3.9. Yet, there is no obligation for the employer to inform the rejected candidate about the individual hired or their qualifications.

Employers must register their employees with the Social Security Institution prior to their work start date.

3.9. Fines and Penalties

Employers who discriminate against an employee/candidate based on their gender or pregnancy will be fined per employee/candidate. The penalty amount varies each year.

Discriminated employees can request compensation per the general principles of the law of obligations. The Labor Code allows discriminated employees to request discrimination compensation—capped at four times their monthly salary—only if the discriminatory conduct occurred during employment or their termination, not during the conclusion of the employment contract. If an employer discriminates against an employee during the conclusion of the employment contract due to union issues, the employee can request union compensation, the minimum of which is one year's salary.

Individuals that have been discriminated against should first inform the relevant party that their behaviors are not in compliance with the Law on the

Turkish Institution of Human Rights and Equality. The relevant party should respond to the allegation within thirty days; if the relevant party objects to or does not respond to the allegation, the individual can apply to the Turkish Institution of Human Rights and Equality. If, on the other hand, damages which are hard or impossible to compensate are likely to arise, the individual can directly apply to the Turkish Institution of Human Rights and Equality. Complaints submitted to the Turkish Institution of Human Rights and Equality during the statutory period for filing a lawsuit cease the filing period for the relevant lawsuit.

If an individual's discrimination allegation is based on Article 5 of the Labor Code, and if they have exhausted the legal remedies foreseen in the Labor Code and the relevant legislation and no decision has been made to impose a sanction, the individual can apply to the Turkish Institution of Human Rights and Equality.

Upon receipt of the discrimination complaint, the Turkish Institution of Human Rights and Equality will advise the parties to settle by request or ex officio. If the parties cannot come to an agreement, the Turkish Institution of Human Rights and Equality will review the complaint and issue a decision. If the individual can provide convincing evidence of the counterparty's discriminatory behavior, the burden of proof to prove otherwise rests on the counterparty.

The employer will face an administrative fine in case of violation of discrimination. The penalty amount varies each year. The Turkish Institution of Human Rights and Equality will file a criminal complaint against violations they deem a crime.

Private-sector workplaces with fifty or more employees must comply with a disabled employee quota equaling 3% of the total number of their employees in the same province. Employers failing to comply with this quota will be subject to an administrative fine for each disabled employee they should have hired, for each month the violation is not rectified. The penalty amount varies each year.

Under the Data Protection Law, the following actions of the employer may be subject to administrative fines:

If the employer fails to fulfill notice requirement with respect to its employees (e.g., regarding its identity, the purpose for processing data, third parties whose data will be transferred to, the method and legal grounds of collection, the rights of the data subject); if the employer fails to comply with the data security obligations; if the employer fails to comply with an order from the Personal Data Protection Board to remedy violations of the Data Protection Law; if the employer fails to register with the Data Controllers Registry. The penalty amounts vary each year.

Criminal penalties may also be assessed against data controllers that unlawfully process or transfer personal data or that fail to delete personal data. The criminal penalties may range from 1 year to 4.5 years of imprisonment under the Turkish Criminal Code. Accordingly, under Article 135 of the Turkish Criminal Code, employees who illegally collect personal data may be subject to imprisonment of 1–3 years. If the personal data is sensitive personal data, the employee may be subject to imprisonment of 1.5–4.5 years. Moreover, according to Article 136 of the Turkish Criminal Code, those who illegally transfer, disseminate, or collect personal data are subject to imprisonment of 2–4 years.

Further, Article 138 of the Turkish Criminal Code sentences employers who fail to delete, destruct, or anonymize their employees' personal data following the termination of the retention period to imprisonment of one to two years. According to Article 140 of the Turkish Criminal Code, if a data privacy crime is committed within the scope or as a result of a legal entity's operations, the relevant entity might be subject to security measures for the relevant crimes. The security measures may be (i) revocation of the license/permit; and/or (ii) confiscation of property or material interests relating to the offense/crime per Article 60 of the Turkish Criminal Code. Under the general principles of the law of obligations, employees can also demand compensation from their employer.

3.10. Checklist of Dos and Do Nots

- Job postings should not discriminate against candidates in any form, such as gender, pregnancy, maternity, union membership, or disabilities. Postings should only list the qualifications and experience necessary for the job.
- Pre-employment inquiries, interviews, and hiring procedures should not discriminate against the candidates.
- Handle candidates' personal data carefully, as their mismanagement can have penal consequences. Obtain written and wet-signed acknowledgments from candidates and employees in Turkish, stating that they have been informed about the processing of their personal data.
- The reasons for not hiring a candidate should be objective and substantiated.
- Ask the correct and appropriate questions to discern whether a candidate is unsuitable or unqualified for the position.

4. MANAGING PERFORMANCE/CONDUCT

4.1. Overview

Employers utilize performance reviews to assess salary raises, promotions, benefits, and termination. The employer can terminate a contract due to valid reasons, including poor performance and misconduct. Temporary or short-term poor performance is not a sufficiently valid reason to terminate the contract. Employers should document their employees' performance or conduct evaluations should they ever be required to utilize the evaluations as evidence for termination based on poor performance or misconduct, or in any legal dispute that may arise between the employer and employee.

4.2. Coaching and Counseling

Employers considering the termination of an employee due to poor performance should offer the employee coaching and counseling services prior to termination. The employer should meet with the employee to discuss the reasons for their poor performance, offer coaching and counseling services, and grant them a reasonable period in which to improve their performance. Employers should design a realistic, target-oriented performance improvement plan to assist the employee. The Supreme Court of Appeals stipulates that performance improvement plans should be a minimum of six months in length. The Supreme Court of Appeals accepts any terminations for poor performance in which the employer did not provide the employee with sufficient additional support to improve their performance invalid.

4.3. Written Evaluations

The Supreme Court of Appeals suggests employers conduct and properly document regular performance reviews to collect evidence of employees' poor performances. The performance review criteria should be objective and applicable to all employees doing the same/similar work.

Performance standards should be in line with the nature of the enterprise and workplace, as well as realistic and sensible. Employers should communicate performance standards to their employees prior to their implementation.

It is vital to document objective performance/conduct reviews in writing, as written evaluations provide strong evidence in the event of a termination contestation, as the Supreme Court of Appeal's suggestion indicates. An original, employee signed copy of the written evaluation should be preserved in the employee's personnel file and another copy should be given to the employee.

4.4. Warnings and Suspensions

Employers should document poor employee performance by issuing written warnings, which can help the employer to initiate a performance improvement plan for the employee.

If the employee's performance does not improve after receiving additional support, as listed in section 4.2., the employer should issue a warning stating the same. The written warning should also state that the employer cannot accept continued poor performance and that the employee may suffer disciplinary consequences, including termination, if their performance does not markedly improve.

Prior to terminating an employee due to poor performance or misconduct, the employer must obtain the employee's written defense. In a reinstatement lawsuit, failure to obtain the employee's written defense will result in the court refusing to examine the merits of the case and rendering the termination invalid.

4.5. Checklist of Dos and Do Nots

- Conduct and document regular performance reviews based on objective criteria.
- Ensure performance standards are appropriate for the nature of the enterprise and the workplace.
- Communicate performance standards to employees prior to their implementation, preferably while beginning employment.
- Conduct performance evaluations in writing and properly document them; they are evidence in the event of termination and/or a legal dispute.
- Prior to termination due to poor performance, communicate with the employee to discuss the reasons for their poor performance, offer coaching and counseling services, and grant them a reasonable period in which to improve their performance.
- Document an employee's poor performance by issuing written warnings. Inform the employee, in writing, that they will be given a performance improvement plan to improve their performance.
- Obtain the employee's written defense prior to terminating them due to poor performance or misconduct.

- Carefully monitor the employee's conduct while on the performance improvement plan. Regularly meet with the employee to evaluate their progress.

5. TERMINATION OF EMPLOYEES FOR PERFORMANCE OR DISCIPLINARY REASONS

5.1. Overview

Turkish law considers employee termination due to poor performance as a valid reason for termination. Termination due to disciplinary issues, depending on the severity of the employee's behavior, may be considered both valid reason and just cause.

5.1.1. Termination of Employees for Performance

Employers can terminate employees for valid reasons which are the employee's incapacity to fulfill their duties or misbehavior (inflicting damage to the employer's property, disloyalty, and tardiness, etc.); and business necessities (such as redundancy or economic, technological, structural, or reorganizational issues) of the enterprise, the business or the work.

Valid reason termination must be an employer's last resort (*ultima ratio*). Employers must have undertaken viable measures prior to termination and alternative ways to refrain from terminating the employee. Such measures include transferring the employee to a more suitable department or role by obtaining the employee's written consent within six business days before enacting the transfer (if required), offering unpaid leave with the employee's prior written consent, or offering further professional training. Termination must be due to objective reasons and not as a means of reducing business expenditures.

Refer to section 4 for the conditions for poor performance termination. Temporary or short-term poor performance is not a valid reason for termination. The employer should meet with the employee to discuss the reasons for their poor performance, give additional support to the employee (offering coaching and counseling services etc.), and grant them a reasonable period in which to improve their performance. The employer should issue the employee with written warnings regarding their poor performance. If the employee's performance does not improve after receiving additional support, the employer should issue a warning stating the same. The written warning should also state that the employer cannot accept continued poor performance and that the employee may suffer disciplinary consequences, including termination, if their performance does not markedly improve.

Prior to terminating an employee due to poor performance, the employer must obtain the employee's written defense, per the Labor Code requirements. Termination due to valid reasons, and thus termination based on poor performance, must be served in writing to ensure the termination's legitimacy. In a reinstatement lawsuit, failure to obtain the employee's written defense will result in the court refusing to examine the merits of the case and rendering the termination invalid.

The written termination notice served to the employee must clearly state the reason for termination. When serving the notice, two other individuals should be present in the event the employee refuses to accept delivery of the notice. The two individuals must sign the notice indicating they witnessed the employee's refusal. The witness signed notice can be delivered to the employee's residence via notary public to further corroborate the evidence.

Termination due to poor performance must be conducted within a reasonable timeframe following the initial observation of the employee's poor performance. A "reasonable timeframe" depends on the circumstances of the termination.

The employer cannot amend their reasons for termination after serving the termination notice, such as in litigation.

5.1.2. Termination of Employees for Disciplinary Reasons

5.1.2.1. Termination for Valid Reason

Per Article 25 of the Labor Code, and as will be discussed in section 5.1.2.2., an employee's misbehavior can constitute a just cause. If, on the other hand, the employee's misbehavior does not qualify as just cause, the employer can terminate the employee with a valid reason as explained in section 5.1.1.

As is the case with other valid reason terminations, disciplinary-based terminations that qualify as valid reasons must be an action of last resort, as delineated in section 5.1.1.

Employers should clearly communicate and document the employee's misbehavior by issuing them written warnings, which should identify the precise behavior contrary to the employer's regulations or the basic norms of employment. If the employee has not improved their behavior after receiving warnings, the employer should issue another written warning asserting the same, that they cannot accept the continued misbehavior, and that the employee may suffer disciplinary consequences, including termination, if their behavior does not markedly improve.

Prior to terminating an employee for a valid reason due to disciplinary reasons, the employer must obtain the employee's written defense, per the Labor Code requirements. In a reinstatement lawsuit, failure to obtain the employee's written defense will result in the court refusing to examine the merits of the case and rendering the termination invalid.

The written termination notice served to the employee must clearly state the reason for termination. When serving the notice, two other individuals should be present in the event the employee refuses to accept delivery of the notice. The two individuals must sign the notice indicating they witnessed the employee's refusal. The witness signed notice can be delivered to the employee's residence via notary public to further corroborate the evidence.

Terminations due to disciplinary reasons must be conducted within a reasonable timeframe following the initial observation of the employee's misbehavior. A "reasonable timeframe" depends on the circumstances of the termination.

The employer cannot amend their reasons for termination after serving the termination notification, such as in litigation.

5.1.2.2. Termination for a Just Cause

Terminations based on disciplinary issues may meet the requirements for just cause, provided that the employer and employee cannot be reasonably expected to perform their duties per the employment contract.

Employers can terminate their employees due to just cause based on four primary circumstances listed in Article 25 of the Labor Code: (1) health reasons; (2) employee behavior contrary to the rules of ethics and goodwill and similar cases; (3) force majeure; and (4) employee's absence due to detention or arrest. Termination for disciplinary reasons may fall under circumstance (2). While these circumstances are not exhaustive, they provide general guidelines for just cause terminations. Particularly, terminations for disciplinary reasons under the scope of the employee's behavior being contrary to the rules of ethics and goodwill and similar cases include the following:

(a) If the employee misled the employer through false claims, statements, or information about their qualifications or conditions necessary to perform their job while concluding the employment contract.
(b) If the employee behaves in a manner offensive to the honor and dignity of the employer or their family members, or makes groundless accusations against the employer that offend the employer's honor and dignity.
(c) If the employee sexually harasses another employee.

(d) If the employee assaults a co-worker, the employer, or a member of the employer's family, or if the employee comes to work while under the influence of alcohol or drugs, or consumes these while in the workplace.
(e) If the employee is disloyal or dishonest to their employer, such as breaching their trust and thieving or disclosing the employer's trade secrets.
(f) If the employee commits a crime in the workplace that merits imprisonment for seven or more days which cannot be delayed.
(g) If the employee is absent from work without the employer's authorization or for a just reason for two consecutive business days or twice in one month on a business day following a holiday or three business days in one month.
(h) If, despite being given warnings, the employee refuses to perform their work functions or responsibilities.
(i) If the employee, deliberately or by gross negligence, jeopardize the safety at the workplace, damages or misplaces the machines, equipment, or other workplace properties and materials belonging to the employer or which are under the employer's possession to such an extent that the damage cannot be compensated by their thirty days' salary.

A termination for just cause must be effected within six business days of detecting the offending behavior and the offender. If the incident requires the collection of further evidence through an investigation, an investigation must be initiated within six business days of detecting the behavior and the offender. When the individual or corporate body authorized to terminate employees within the employer entity is notified of the investigation results, the termination must be effected within six business days of their receipt of the investigation results. The employer, however, cannot terminate the employment agreement based on "employee's behavior contradicting the rules of ethics, goodwill, and similar incidents" if the termination is not exercised within six business days from the employer's discovery of such grounds, and in any case, one year after the occurrence of such event. The one-year period is not applicable if the employee has obtained a monetary benefit from the act potentially giving rise to the termination.

The written notice of termination for just cause is a matter of proof, not validity, differently from termination with valid reason; as such, the notice can take any form. It is advisable that the notification be issued in clear written form.

An exception to the above is the termination of union representatives or managers. Terminating a union representative or manager, in principle, requires a just cause, and termination must be done through a written notice clearly articulating the just cause.

The employer cannot amend their reasons for termination after serving the termination notification, such as in litigation.

5.2. SEPARATION/SEVERANCE PAY

When terminating an employee for a valid reason or just cause, the employee's compensation package must include:

- Accrued salary as of the termination date.
- Accrued bonuses/commissions, if any, as of the termination date.
- Accrued untaken annual leave pay, if any, as of the termination date.
- Accrued overtime/exceeding time pay.
- Accrued pay for work on national, public holidays, and at weekends, if any.
- All other employee contractual entitlements.

Additional payments vary based on whether termination is due to valid reason or just cause.

5.2.1. Termination for Valid Reason

5.2.1.1. Notice Compensation (İhbar Tazminatı)

An employee terminated due to a valid reason must be paid notice and statutory seniority compensation, as well as all accrued statutory and contractual entitlements. A statutory notice period is based on the terminated employee's length of employment:

(a) For up to six months of employment: two weeks.
(b) For six months to a year and a half of employment: four weeks.
(c) For a year and a half to three years of employment: six weeks.
(d) For more than three years of employment: eight weeks.

Notice periods can be contractually negotiated. Settled case laws provide that only the employer and not the employee is bound by the increased contractual notice periods longer than statutory notice periods. In other words, the employee will be subject to the aforementioned statutory notice periods, which differs between two and eight weeks depending on the employee's period of service.

Failure on the terminating party's behalf to provide the required notice results in their requirement to pay notice compensation to the terminated party. Notice compensation is calculated by multiplying the days of the required notice period by the employee's latest daily gross salary. In this calculation, the employee's daily gross salary must include additional benefits such as car allowance, gas allowance, meal allowance, and private health insurance (*giydirilmiş brüt ücret*).

5.2.1.2. Statutory Seniority Compensation (Kıdem Tazminatı)

Individuals employed for longer than one year who are terminated for reasons other than their behavior being contrary to the rules of ethics and goodwill and similar cases are, in principle, entitled to statutory seniority compensation.

Statutory compensation is calculated by multiplying the employee's latest monthly gross salary (*giydirilmiş brüt ücret*), including all additional benefits provided beyond the gross salary, and the terminated individual's years of employment.

The Ministry sets the maximum amount in terms of the monthly gross salary amount, which should be taken into consideration for calculating the statutory seniority compensation payable amount. In other words, even if the employee's monthly gross salary is higher than such announced maximum amount, the announced maximum amount will be taken as basis for the employee's monthly gross salary while calculating the statutory seniority compensation.

For the first six months of 2022 (the period between January 1, 2022 and June 30, 2022), the maximum monthly gross salary amount for the purposes of calculating the statutory seniority compensation was TRY 10,848.59. The maximum monthly gross salary amount for the purposes of calculating the statutory seniority compensation for the second six months of 2022 (the period between July 1, 2022 and December 31, 2022) has been announced as TRY 15,371.40.

5.2.2. Termination for Just Cause

Employers are not required to pay notice compensation in just cause terminations. The employment relationship is immediately terminated. Furthermore, employers are not required to pay statutory seniority compensation in just cause terminations due to the employee's behavior contrary to the rules of ethics and goodwill and similar cases. For other just cause terminations such as health reasons, however, the employer is required to pay statutory seniority compensation to the employee.

Section 5.2.1.2. specifies the calculation for statutory seniority compensation.

5.3. Fines and Penalties

A terminated employee has the right to request reinstatement if the employers do not complete the procedures detailed in sections 5.1.1. and 5.1.2. and if the employee meets the additional reinstatement conditions below:

- The workplace employs thirty or more employees.[1]
- The employment agreement must be for an indefinite term.
- The employee must work with the employer for at least six months.[2]
- The employee must be an ordinary employee, i.e., not an "employer's representative" authorized to manage the entire enterprise or their assistant (*işveren vekili veya yardımcısı*), or an "employer's representative" managing the entire workplace who is also authorized to recruit and terminate employees.

In reinstatement lawsuits, the burden of proof for just cause or valid reason termination lies with the employer. Prior to termination, therefore, the employer must certify that they have obtained the relevant necessary documentation to justify the termination. Turkish courts, which overwhelmingly tend to side with employees, value hard copy documentation written in Turkish.

If the employee wins the reinstatement lawsuit, the employer must reinstate the employee and pay nonemployment compensation (*boşta geçen sürelere ilişkin ücret*) equaling up to four times the employee's monthly gross salary. The monthly gross salary amount for this calculation must include all additional employee benefit amounts (*giydirilmiş brüt ücret*).

If the employee is not reinstated, the employer must pay non-reinstatement compensation *(işe başlatmama tazminatı)*, which totals four to eight months of the employee's monthly base gross salary (net salary, social security premiums, and taxes), as well as nonemployment compensation. If the employer reinstates the employee, they are not required to pay this non-reinstatement compensation.

1. The total number of employees is calculated based on the total number of employees in all related business workplaces if the employer has multiple workplaces in the same line of business. In case where a company with foreign capital, a branch office or a liaison office is the employing entity, the Supreme Court of Appeals tends to assume that this criterion has been satisfied.
2. If the employee previously worked with the employer, their prior length of employment is added to calculate the total seniority.

If the employer did not pay notice and statutory seniority compensations during termination, the employer must ensure their payment thereafter. The employer is responsible for the payment of additional items such as court fees, statutory attorney fees, interest, increases in the annual paid leave day, if any, increases in the notice compensation entitlement, if any, increases in the statutory seniority compensation entitlement and up to four months' worth of social security premiums.

5.4. Checklist of Dos and Do Nots

- If considering terminating an employee due to poor performance, provide them with additional support—such as coaching, periodic meetings, and training—prior to termination. Grant the employee sufficient time to improve their performance.
- Issue written warnings to employees exhibiting poor performance or misbehavior as a means of documenting the situation.
- If the employee's performance/behavior does not improve after receiving additional support and/or issuance of warning letter, the employer should issue an additional warning stating the same. The written warning should also state that the employer cannot accept continued poor performance/misbehavior and that the employee may suffer disciplinary consequences, including termination, if their performance/behavior does not markedly improve.
- Prior to terminating an employee due to a valid reason based on poor performance or misbehavior, obtain the employee's written defense. It is crucial to issue a written termination notice that explicitly states the reasons for terminations to the employee.
- If the employee refuses to accept the written termination notice, have two witnesses sign the notice and mail it to the employee's residence via notary.
- Terminations for valid reasons should be effected within a reasonable period following the recognition of the employee's poor performance or misbehavior.
- Terminations for valid reasons must be an employer's last resort (*ultima ratio*).
- Observe the six business days' rule for terminations based on just cause.
- Although not legally required for terminations based on just cause, it is advisable to serve employees with a written termination notice for evidentiary purposes.
- The employer is bound by and cannot amend their reasons for termination after serving the termination notification.

- Employers should exercise additional prudence when terminating union representatives or managers.
- Turkish labor courts are extremely pro-employee.
- In reinstatement lawsuits, the employer must prove the existence of a valid reason or just cause for termination.

6. LAYOFFS, REDUCTIONS IN FORCE, AND/OR REDUNDANCIES AS A RESULT OF JOB ELIMINATIONS OR OTHER RESTRUCTURINGS

6.1. Overview

The employer has the right to take the operational decisions they deem appropriate for the enterprise, workplace, and work since the employer assumes the risks associated with those decisions.

The Turkish Constitution constitutes the legal basis of the employer's right to make operational decisions by stating that everyone has the right and duty to work. In principle, employers' operational decisions are not conditional on judicial review or approval. However, operational decisions that result in employment termination will be judicially reviewed to determine their necessity.

6.2. Reductions in Force/Layoffs/Job Eliminations

Turkish law determines that the business necessities (redundancy or economic, technological, structural, or reorganizational issues, etc.) of the enterprise, workplace, or work are valid reasons for employment termination. Business necessities tend to be economic difficulties, such as portfolio loss, work volume decrease, economic crises, reorganization, and redundancies due to technological developments or reorganization.

Terminations due to business necessities require the employer to prove that carrying out their operational decision necessitated objective employee termination and that the business decision was a valid reason for termination. Business necessities terminations must be due to objective reasons and not as a means of reducing business expenditures. Employers must issue a board decision delineating the employer's extenuating economic circumstances, and how these circumstances have left the employer with no choice but to terminate employees. The board decision should include termination details such as the timeline, departments, positions, and the number of affected employees. The decision should be applied consistently and impartially to demonstrate the veracity of the reasons for termination.

Employers must ascertain that their financial books abide by the board decision considering that in reinstatement lawsuits initiated due to business necessities terminations, courts appoint experts to review the employer's financial books to corroborate the legitimacy of the business necessities resulting in employee termination.

As with other valid reasons, terminations due to business necessity must be an employer's last resort (*ultima ratio*). Employers should have undertaken less forceful measures for improvement prior to termination such as transferring employees to more suitable departments or roles or offering unpaid leave by obtaining the employee's written consent within six business days before enacting the measures, and shortening working hours, or ceasing overtime.

If the employer has executed a collective bargaining contract, they must comply with the termination procedures within the contract. Failure to comply with the contractual procedures could invalidate termination and result in administrative fines. In fact, collective bargaining contracts generally provide termination procedures due to business necessities and collective terminations.

Collective termination procedure is particularly regulated by the Labor Code which also covers employers' rights to terminate employees for business necessities. Collective termination is when the employer terminates, on the same date or on different dates but within the same month:

- at least 10 employees in a workplace of 20–100 employees;
- at least 10% of employees in a workplace of 101–300 employees; or
- at least 30 employees in a workplace of 301 or more employees.

Such thresholds will be observed on a workplace basis, at which the collective termination will occur and employees of subcontractors *(alt işveren işçileri)* and employees engaged in temporary employment relationships *(geçici iş ilişkisi)* are not included in the above thresholds.

Collective termination due to economic, technical, organizational, or similar reasons require the employer to submit written notifications thereof to the workplaces' union representative and the Regional Directorate of Labor and Turkish Employment Institution (the "Regional Directorate") a minimum of thirty days before the termination. The written notifications must include the reasons for termination, the timeline for the termination and details of the terminated employees (numbers and groups). Employers must also provide the terminated employees with a written notification.

Employee termination notices are effective thirty days after the submission of notice to the Regional Directorate. The employer and workplace union representative must meet after the notifications are submitted to the representative and the Regional Directorate. The meeting is merely consultative: they will discuss how to prevent collective termination, decrease the number of terminations, and minimize the termination's negative effects on the employees. Meeting minutes must be prepared and signed.

If a workplace is shut down and the activities therein are ceased, definitely and permanently, the employer must only make a workplace announcement and notify the Regional Directorate at least thirty days prior. As a best practice, it is recommended to notify the workplace union representatives about the workplace closure as well, at least thirty days prior. In this case, too, employers must provide the terminated employees with a written notification by respecting the abovementioned thirty days' waiting period.

If within six months of the collective termination finalization the employer intends to hire individuals for the same work, they must offer the positions to their previous qualified employees. If the employees accept, the employer must rehire them.

In business necessities terminations, the employer must pay the terminated employees notice and statutory seniority compensations, and accrued contractual and other statutory entitlements.

6.3. Fines and Penalties

Employers who do not comply with the collective termination procedure will be subject to an administrative fine per terminated employee. The penalty amount varies each year.

If the employer has executed a collective bargaining contract, they must comply with the termination procedures within the contract. Failure to comply with the contractual procedures could invalidate termination and result in administrative fines.

If employers do not comply with the Labor Code and collective bargaining agreement procedures on terminations, labor courts could accept terminated employees' reinstatement lawsuits.

6.4. Checklist of Dos and Do Nots

- Termination due to business necessities must not be arbitrary, based on objective criteria, and not to reduce expenses.
- Employers must introduce a board decision explaining the employer's extenuating economic reasons for terminating employees. The decision must be applied consistently and impartially to demonstrate the veracity of the reasons for termination.
- Employers must consider all possibilities prior to terminating due to business necessities, as this is a last resort (*ultima ratio*).

- Employers should heed the termination procedures in collective bargaining contracts.
- In collective terminations, the affected employees and relevant authorities must be duly and punctually notified. Procedures must be properly enacted, as failing to do so results in fines and could invalidate the terminations.

7. LABOR AND EMPLOYMENT LAW RAMIFICATIONS UPON ACQUISITION OR SALE OF A BUSINESS

7.1. Overview

The Labor Code sets forth the workplace transfer and their effects on employment contracts while the Turkish Commercial Code No. 6102, effective since July 1, 2012 (the "Commercial Code") also introduces special provisions regarding the transfer of employment contracts following mergers, acquisitions, demergers, and corporate law company structure changes.

7.2. Acquisition/Merger of a Business

According to the Commercial Code, the employees whose employing company underwent a merger or acquisition have the right to object to the merger or acquisition. This right is applicable to transactions in which the merging companies' assets are transferred (instead of liquidated) to the acquired company, i.e., mergers by acquisition or mergers by way of new establishment.

An employee's objection to a merger or acquisition does not immobilize the merger or acquisition process, but it does allow the employee to impede the transfer of their employment contract to the transferee employer and terminate their employment at the end of their notice period. The transferor employer and the employee, or the transferee employer and employee if the merger or acquisition was registered prior to the end of the employee's notice period, must fulfill their duties under the employment contract until the end of the notice period.

Scholars opine that employees objecting to the transfer of their employment to a transferee employer due to merger or acquisition should receive paid statutory seniority compensation albeit they are the ones terminating their contract.

The Commercial Code applies the above principles *mutatis mutandis* to the demergers and corporate structure changes defined therein.

7.3. Acquisition Checklist

- Evaluate the target company's employment contracts and internal regulations and policies.
- Evaluate any existing collective bargaining contracts; if said contracts require, hold a meeting with union representatives.
- Assess the financial and corporate aspects of the planned business and management reorganization.
- Inform and obtain the consent of the employees affected by the merger or acquisition.
- Institute recourse mechanisms for obligations that could develop due to the transferor employer's inability to perform their liabilities for employment contracts.
- Supply or acquire guarantees to fulfill any requested employees' due receivables.

7.4. Sale of a Business

Article 6 of the Labor Code views the sale of a business as a type of workplace transfer. The identification of whether a workplace was transferred to another employer, particularly if a section of the workplace was transferred to a third party, relies on the principle of economic integrity.

According to the Supreme Court of Appeals, the transfer of a business, wholly or in part, which preserves its economic integrity constitutes a workplace transfer.

The business integrity criteria vary and are determined on a case-by-case basis. For instance, workplaces whose primary activity is manufacturing and production rely on the transfer of material assets as the criteria to ascertain whether the sale of their business is a workplace transfer. Workplaces whose primary activity is the provision of a service rely on the assessment of their know-how, patents, licenses, and labor to ascertain whether the sale of their business is a workplace transfer.

Employment relationships are not affected by the whole or partial transfer of a workplace. Employment contracts are, in principle, transferred with the workplace and continue to be valid and exercisable in the same conditions as before the transfer. The debts and rights under employment contracts are due on the transfer date. Transferred employees cannot object to the transfer of their employment.

The transferor and transferee employers are jointly and severally liable for employees' receivables that have arisen prior to and due on the transfer date. The transferor employer's liability with respect to such liabilities, however, lasts for two years as of the transfer date. The transferor and transferee employers generally execute an agreement or regulate a recourse mechanism in the corporate agreements with regard to such liabilities. These recourse mechanisms can however not be imposed on the employees.

Employment contracts cannot be terminated—by the transferor employer, transferee employer, or the employees—due to the whole or partial workplace transfer. The transferor or transferee employers must have an economic, technological, or corporate organization reason for termination. The parties' right to terminate the employment agreement with just cause is reserved.

7.5. Sale Checklist

- Prior to the transaction, evaluate the relevant and effective employment agreements and collective bargaining agreements. If so required under a collective bargaining contract, hold an explanatory meeting with union representatives.
- Assess the financial and corporate aspects of the planned business and management reorganization.

8. USE OF ALTERNATIVE WORKFORCES: INDEPENDENT CONTRACTORS, CONTRACT EMPLOYEES, AND TEMPORARY OR LEASED WORKERS, TELECOMMUTING

8.1. Overview

Turkish employers often utilize alternative workforces, such as subcontractors, temporary employment, and leased workers, to perform a part of the entire work necessitating expertise. Hiring external employees is pragmatic, as it can decrease costs and expenses. The Labor Code regulates subcontracting, leased workers, and telecommuting.

Turkish employment law provides statutory principles to protect the rights of subcontracted employees. Employers can engage independent contractors under certain circumstances and cannot do so merely to decrease their expenses.

8.2. Independent Contractors

Under Turkish labor laws, subcontracting is a form of independent contracting. The employer, known as the Principal Employer, can obtain from another employer, known as the Subcontractor, specific works or services. Article 4 of the Subcontracting Regulation stipulates certain criteria for the execution of a subcontracting agreement:

(a) The Principal Employer must also employ their own employees working in the production of goods or services at their own workplace.
(b) The subcontracted work must be considered side work in the overall production of goods and services for the principal workplace, such as catering, transportation, and cleaning services. Principal work that is apportioned and assigned to a Subcontractor must originate from the specifics of the work or enterprise and must be due to technical necessity.
(c) The Subcontractor's employees must only work in the workplace specified under the subcontracting agreement.
(d) The Subcontractor can only perform work dependent on the continuance of and related to the principal work and the manufacturing of the goods and services.
(e) The Subcontractor cannot be an individual the Principal Employer had employed prior.

A business' side works, in principle, e.g., catering, transportation, and security can be subcontracted without restrictions. Sections of the principal businesses can only be assigned to a Subcontractor due to a business necessity (*işin ve işletmenin gereği*) and technical necessity (*teknolojik gereklilik*).

Article 10 of the Subcontracting Regulation requires the inclusion of certain information in a subcontracting agreement:

(a) The Principal Employer and Subcontractor's workplace titles and addresses.
(b) The Principal Employer and Subcontractor's legal entity titles; if they do not have legal entities, the names, surnames, and addresses of the employers' representatives.
(c) The scope of the principal business carried out in the Principal Employer's workplace.
(d) The scope of the work assigned to the Subcontractor.
(e) A technical explanation, based on technical and business necessities, why a section of the principal work was assigned to the Subcontractor.
(f) The agreed dates for the commencement and conclusion of the subcontracted work.
(g) The area of the workplace where the Subcontractor will carry out their business.

(h) Assertion that, as per Article 2 of the Labor Code, the Principal Employer and Subcontractor are jointly and severally liable for obligations towards the Subcontractor's employees regarding the workplace and resulting from the law, employment agreement, or collective bargaining the Subcontractor has executed.
(i) Assertion that the rights of the workers employed by the Principal Employer prior to the execution of the subcontracting agreement and later employed by the Subcontractor cannot be restricted.
(j) Guidelines of how the Subcontractor should perform their assigned work.
(k) The signatures of the Principal Employer or their representative, and the Subcontractor or their representative.

The remedies for violating Article 10 are not supplied in the Subcontracting Regulation.

If any of the Principal Employer's employees are transferred to the Subcontractor, and if they continue to work at the principal workplace, their rights, and benefits cannot be altered to their detriment.

The subcontracting agreement is collusive if the subcontracting relationship seeks to eliminate the Principal Employer's primary liabilities or detrimentally diminish their employees' benefits while the employees continue to work under the Principal Employer's supervision. Pursuant to the Labor Code and Subcontracting Regulation, a subcontracting agreement can be accepted collusive if:

(a) the Principal Employer assigns the Subcontractor work that does not fall in the scope of side work;
(b) the work assigned to the Subcontractor is part of the primary business, but does not require any expertise per the technical necessities or business necessities;
(c) the Subcontractor was previously employed in the Principal Employer's workplace;
(d) the Subcontractor lacks the suitable equipment or experience to perform the assigned work;
(e) the Subcontractor's employees lack the adequate qualifications to execute the assigned work;
(f) the Principal Employer utilizes employees for the assigned work other than the ones appointed to coordinate and supervise the Subcontractor's assigned works;
(g) the Principal Employer executes the subcontracting agreement to circumvent their legally imposed obligations, such as to avoid the liabilities associated with occupational health and safety regulations or decrease the number of employees in the workplace; and

(h) the Principal Employer executes the subcontracting agreement to circumvent their liabilities or to detrimentally diminish their employees' individual or collective rights and benefits stemming from their employment agreements, collective bargaining agreements, or the relevant law.

If a subcontracting relationship is deemed collusive, the Subcontractor's registration will be revoked and their employees will be considered the Principal Employer's employees from the beginning of the subcontracting relationship. Both the Principal Employer and the Subcontractor will be fined administrative fines due to the collusive subcontracting relationship as long as it continues.

Employers must not utilize subcontracting as a means to cut costs: companies in solid financial health, in need for technological development or corporate reorganization must not subcontract employees to cut costs or employ subcontracted employees at lower salaries rather than utilizing their own contracted employees.

A subcontracting agreement's length is limited to the term of necessity. A company, for instance, suffering from economic difficulties that engages in subcontracting should terminate the relationship when it has resolved said difficulties.

Works assigned to the Subcontractor requiring technical proficiency and that are crucial to the business' operation must have a list of work equipment, work completion certificate, and operator and technical staff certificates attached to the subcontracting agreement. These documents are utilized to prove that the Subcontractor's technical capabilities are sufficient to complete the assigned work.

The Principal Employer must ensure that the Subcontractor pays their employees' salaries and social security premiums. If the Principal Employer concludes that the Subcontractor has defaulted salary payments, they must deduct the salary amounts from the payments they make the Subcontractor and deposit them directly to the employees' bank accounts.

The Subcontractor must register the subcontracting agreement and subcontracted employees to work in the Principal Employer's workplace with the Social Security Institution. The subcontracting agreement must be submitted to the Regional Directorate, and as such, the Principal Employer must ensure it includes the legally required information in the agreement.

8.3. Contract Workers

Contract workers that meet the conditions stipulated in the Labor Code are considered employees of the Principal Employer or the Subcontractor.

8.4. Temporary and Leased Workers, Telecommuting

Temporary Employment Relationships

With the employee's prior written consent, the employer can temporarily assign the employee to another employer within the same group of companies or holding for a maximum of six months. Article 7 of the Labor Code allows the six-month period to be extended, for the same length, twice.

The permanent employer assigned the employee to another employer is responsible for paying the assigned employee's salary. The temporary employer, along with the permanent employer, is jointly and severally liable for the assigned employee's unpaid salary and social security premiums.

Leased Workers

In 2016, Turkey recognized the agency worker structure presented by the European Union Directive 2008/104/EC. The Law on Amending the Labor Code and the Turkey Labor Institution Code No. 6715 (the "Law No. 6715") entered into force on May 20, 2016 and allowed private employment agencies to lease employees to other companies under certain circumstances.

The amended Labor Code allows for the leasing of personnel for certain works:

(a) due to the situations listed in Article 13, paragraph 5 (employee's right to request to be transferred postnatal part-time work) and Article 74 (maternity leave), as well as employee absence due to military service or other cases where the employment agreement is suspended;
(b) due to seasonal agricultural works;
(c) in domestic services;
(d) irregular works not considered part of the workplace's daily business;
(e) urgent works resulting from occupational health and safety concerns, or force majeure reasons that greatly affected production;
(f) an unanticipated and substantial increase in the average production capacity of goods and services requiring the hiring of additional, temporary personnel; and
(g) periodic workload increases, except for seasonal works.

A temporary employment relationship can be initiated for the duration of the conditions under point (a), without a time limit for the conditions under points (b) and (c), and for a maximum of four months for the conditions under points (d), (e), (f), and (g).

A temporary employment agreement can be renewed twice, not exceeding eight months in total, for all cases except for the condition under point (g).

For point (f), an employer can use leased workers equaling to a maximum of 25% of its total employees.

Headhunting companies (also known as payroll companies) licensed by the Turkey Labor Institution can act as intermediaries to connect employers and job candidates. In Turkey, a company cannot act as a payroll company and hire its employees just to lease them to other companies by preserving the employees' labor-related burdens. In such disputes, the Turkish labor courts consider the employer as the company de facto utilizing the employee and not the entity acting as a payroll company.

The definition of a private employment agency was revised by the Turkey Labor Institution Code. A private employment agency can be founded by a real person or a legal entity to provide intermediary services in recruiting job applicants for diverse positions, whether full-time or temporary. A private employment agency must be approved by the Turkey Labor Institution, in order to both provide intermediary services and enter into temporary employment relationships.

In temporary employment relationships, the employer is the private employment agency. Temporary employment relationships are initiated when the private employment agency and the temporary employee execute an employment agreement and the private employment agency and the employer execute a services agreement.

Telecommuting (Remote Working)

With Law No. 6715, the Labor Code's provisions on telecommuting (i.e., remote working) were amended. Accordingly, telecommuting is regulated and defined by Article 14 of the Labor Code, as an employment relationship in which the employees perform their work remotely at home (or outside of the workplace), within the scope of the working organization provided by the employer, through technological communication tools.

In addition to the provision in the Labor Code, Remote Working Regulation (the "Regulation") entered into force on March 10, 2021. The Regulation introduces the details of procedures and principles of remote working. Accordingly, the Regulation regulates in detail the following matters: (i) the form and the content of the agreement related to remote working, (ii) arrangement of the working environment, (iii) supplying and using materials and working tools; covering the production costs; (iv) determination of working periods and communication of the employee with the employer, (v) data protection, (vi) taking measures regarding occupational health and safety, (vii) occupations that cannot be performed remotely, and (viii) transition to remote working.

As regulated in the Regulation, the employment relationship can be established directly with a remote working agreement, or if the employee and employer agree, the employee's employment agreement can be converted into a remote working agreement. If remote working will be applied to the whole or part of the workplace for compelling reasons, the employee's request or approval will not be sought for the transition to remote working.

In the written protocol/agreement related to remote working, the following provisions must be included:

- the description of the work;
- the method of carrying out the work;
- the term and place of work;
- matters regarding the salary and the payment of the salary;
- equipment/working tools provided by the employer and the employee's obligation to protect such equipment/working tools;
- the employer's communication with the employee;
- general and specific working conditions;
- arrangements regarding the location of remote working and the method of covering the costs arising from such arrangements;
- the party that provides the materials required for the production of goods and services and the principles of use of such materials and their maintenance and repair conditions;
- list of working tools provided by the employer;
- issues related to determining and covering the necessary expenses directly related to the production of goods and services arising from the performance of the work;
- time interval and duration of the remote working;
- provisions regarding working hours/overtime work of the employee;
- communication management and the time interval of the communication;
- definition and scope of data to be protected.

The violation of provisions related to remote working may result in an administrative fine. The penalty amount varies each year.

(a) Main Principles of Remote Working

- Employees working remotely cannot be treated differently in comparison to employees who do not carry out work remotely but have the same or similar qualifications and do the same or similar work.
- Remote working is not a justified reason to make substantial changes to the employee's working conditions.
- If necessary, arrangements regarding the location of remote working will be completed before the work starts. The method of covering the costs arising from such arrangements will be determined jointly by the employee and the employer.

- The time interval and duration of remote working must be specified in the agreement related to remote working. The method and time interval of communication in remote working will be determined by the employee and the employer.
- The parties may change the working hours and parties may agree on overtime work to be carried out upon the written request of the employer, in accordance with the employee's consent and legislative provisions.
- During remote working, the rules regarding the arrangement of the working environment and covering the costs, the delivery of the materials and working tools and the related expenses and the payment of the invoices are determined by the parties.
- It is essential that the materials and work tools required for the production of goods and services of the employee are provided by the employer, unless otherwise agreed in the agreement related to remote working. The principles of use and maintenance and repair conditions of these materials and working tools will be communicated clearly to the employee. In addition, the employer must deliver to the employee a list of working tools stating their price on the date of delivery.
- Employer must inform the employee about the business rules and the relevant legislation regarding the protection and sharing of data regarding the workplace and the work and must take the necessary measures to protect such data.

(b) Employee's Request for Transition to Remote Working

The employee must submit his/her request to work remotely in writing to the employer. The employee's request will be evaluated by the employer in line with the procedure specified in the workplace. While evaluating the request, the employer will consider if the request is suitable due to the nature of the occupation and the employee and other criteria determined by the employer. The employee must be notified of the request's evaluation result within thirty days. An employee transferred to remote working can later request to work at their workplace again. The employer will consider the request as a priority. In the event that remote working will be applied in the whole or part of the workplace due to compelling reasons specified in the legislation, the employee's request or approval is not required for the transition to remote work.

(c) Written Consent to Stop Providing Food and Transportation Allowances

The employer cannot, without obtaining the employee's prior written consent, unilaterally stop providing food and transportation allowances to employees working remotely, since such unilateral change will likely be considered a substantial change to the employee's working conditions, to the detriment of the employee. Therefore, the employer must submit a written request to the employee to stop providing these allowances. The employer cannot stop providing these benefits if the employee does not accept this request in writing and within six business days. Otherwise, the employee may terminate the employment agreement based on just cause and demand statutory seniority compensation from the employer.

(d) Health and Safety

The company is liable for the employee's health and safety also while they perform remote working. Although the employer is not required to inspect the place(s) in which the employee intends to work, it would be recommended to do so in order to ensure a safe working environment since the employer has liability with respect to occupational health and safety-related issues. Furthermore, the employer must, by taking into account the nature of the work provided to the employee, inform the employee about the occupational health and safety measures, give him/her the necessary occupational health and safety trainings, safeguard the employee's health and take the necessary occupational safety measures relating to the equipment it provides to the employee.

If the employee has a disease/injury due to the work they carry out, this would be considered an occupational accident/occupational disease and the employer would have liability. However, not every accident that occurs during remote working would be an occupational accident, as the accident needs to relate to the work that the employee performs.

In order to limit the employer's risk exposure, the employer could provide (in the written agreement to be signed between the parties with respect to remote working) a list of the locations, where the employee can work remotely and ask the employee to inform the employer and their manager about a change in their remote working location, in case the employee switches from one of the listed workplaces to another. Since the employer has liability (as explained above) with respect to occupational health and safety-related issues, limiting the places, where the employee can work remotely, could be helpful to limit the employer's risks in terms of occupational health and safety.

Employers are required to declare the number of remote working days of each of their employees, each month to the Social Security Institution. Noncompliance with the obligation to declare the number of remote working days might result in administrative fines for employers.

8.5. Checklist of Dos and Do Nots

- The company's primary business must not be outsourced to subcontractors unless there are business and technical necessities.
- The employer must ascertain that the subcontractor or payroll company complies with labor and social security rules, e.g., they duly register the subcontracting agreement with the relevant authorities and pay the employees' social security premiums.
- Insert recourse mechanisms for potential penalties, fines, and employee claims in all agreements executed with subcontractors and payroll companies.
- Contemplate executing temporary employment relationships brokered via private employment agencies to reduce headcount.
  _ Agreements related to remote working must be made in writing and include aforementioned provisions.
  _ The employer is liable for the employee's health and safety also while they perform remote working.
  _ Notify employees of any substantial changes to their working conditions in writing and obtain the employees' written and wet-signed consent in remote working as well.
- An employee transferred to remote working can later request to work at their workplace again. Consider such request as a priority.

9. OBLIGATION TO BARGAIN COLLECTIVELY WITH TRADE UNIONS: EMPLOYEES' RIGHT TO STRIKE AND A COMPANY'S RIGHT TO CONTINUE BUSINESS OPERATIONS

9.1. Overview of Unions' Right to Organize

Article 51 of the Turkish Constitution grants employees and employers the right to freely establish, become members of or withdraw membership from unions and organizations that protect and cultivate their economic and social rights, as well as their interests in labor relations, without any permission. An individual cannot be forced to initiate or withdraw membership from a union.

Articles 53 and 54 of the Turkish Constitution also set forth collective bargaining agreements, strikes, and lockouts. The Unions Law regulates the procedures of collective bargaining agreements.

9.2. Right of Employees to Join Unions

Employees have a constitutional right to join unions. In this regard, an employee can choose: (i) to establish or join a union and participate in their activities or (ii) to not join a union or participate in their activities.

Article 25 of the Unions Law reiterates this right, adding that employers cannot discriminate against union member employees or terminate their agreements due to union activities or association. Employers failing to abide by these provisions may be ruled to pay compensation equivalent to no less than the relevant employee's annual salary.

9.3. How Employees Select Unions

The Unions Law states that unions are allowed to conduct their activities within their own line of business, such as metals, mining, or construction. The Regulation on Business Lines determines the categories of lines of business:

(a) Hunting, fishing, agriculture, and forestry.
(b) Food industry.
(c) Mining and stone quarry.
(d) Petrol, chemical, rubber, plastic, and pharmacy.
(e) Clothing, readymade clothing, and leather.
(f) Tree and paper.
(g) Communication.
(h) Press, broadcast, and journalism.
(i) Banking, finance, and insurance.
(j) Commerce, office, education, and fine arts.
(k) Cement, soil, and glass.
(l) Metal.
(m) Construction.
(n) Energy.
(o) Transportation.
(p) Shipbuilding and sea transportation, storage and warehousing.
(q) Health and social services.
(r) Accommodation and entertainment business.
(s) Defense and security.
(t) General works.

Union membership is optional and voluntary.

Article 17 of the Unions Laws requires employees to fulfill two requirements to become a union member:

(1) the employee can be a member of only one union within the same line of business; and
(2) the employee must be at least 15 years of age.

If an employee works in a line of business that has more than one union, they must choose to join only one of those unions. Employees who work at several different workplaces simultaneously can join more than one union as long as these unions represent different lines of businesses.

Employees must submit their membership application through the *e-Devlet* website ("e-State" in English). The union's authorized body reviews the employee's application; if the authorized body approves the application, not rejecting the application within thirty days of their submission results in the same, the employee is inducted as a union member. If the application is rejected without just reason, the employee applicant can initiate a lawsuit with the labor court within thirty days of the rejection notification. The labor court's such decision is final and cannot be appealed. If the labor court rules in favor of the applicant, they become a union member retroactively from the date of their application's rejection.

9.4. Pre-election Campaigning

Unions conduct activities to assist and safeguard their member's interests before the employers, such as:

- carry out collective bargaining agreement negotiations;
- in the event of collective disputes, file claims with the relevant authority, labor court, mediator, arbitration board, or other judicial organs; and
- resolve and direct strikes and lockouts.

For a union to be able to execute a collective bargaining agreement with an employer, the union's members must constitute 1% of the employees in their line of business in Turkey.

Additionally, the union must have as members more than 50% of employees working in the same workplace if the union would like to organize within such workplace only. Alternatively, if the employer company has several active workplaces in the same line of business and the union would like to execute a collective bargaining agreement with the employer covering these multiple workplaces, at least 40% of the total number of employees working in the same line of business in the whole employer company must be union members.

Unions must submit an application to the Ministry requesting their authority to execute a collective bargaining agreement with employers. Parties can challenge the Ministry's decision in labor courts within six business days of receiving the decision. The labor court issues its decision within six business days, which can be appealed with the Supreme Court of Appeals. The Supreme Court of Appeals issues their decision within fifteen days. In practice, however, the litigation process takes much more time, due to the workload of the courts.

Collective bargaining agreements must be executed in writing. In principle, only member union employees benefit from the collective bargaining agreement between their union and employer. Nonunion member employees in the respective workplace can, however, choose to pay a solidarity fee to the union in order to benefit from the collective bargaining agreement executed with their employer.

Collective bargaining agreements generally stipulate employment agreement content, terminations, the rights and responsibilities of parties, augmented employee benefits, and the performance and regulation of the agreement. Collective bargaining agreements must be a minimum of one year and a maximum of three years.

9.5. Unfair Labor Practices

Employees' employment agreements suspend when they become trade union managers. The Unions Laws also provide such employees with the right to terminate employment effective immediately and without provision of any notice and to receive statutory seniority compensation upon termination (calculated based on their salary on the termination date). If the employee's agreement is suspended and not terminated, and they are terminated as the trade union manager (due to the union's disincorporation, the employee not being reelected for the position, the employee not participating in the election, or resigning from the position), the employee can request their employer rehire them within one month from their termination as trade union manager. If the employer does not rehire the employee under the same or similar employment terms and conditions within one month from the employee's request, the employer will be deemed to have effectively terminated the employee.

The Unions Law and Labor Code prohibit employers from discriminating against union members regarding candidate selection, work conditions, or employment termination. Candidate recruitment cannot be based on the candidate's decision to join, refrain from joining, withdrawing from, or not applying for membership to any trade union. Similarly, employers cannot discriminate between employees who are union members, nonunion members, or members of different trade unions regarding their working conditions or employment termination. Employers must not discriminate against or base a termination on an employee's union membership or lack thereof, or their participation or performance of union/organization activities outside of working hours or during the employer-sanctioned working hours with the employer's permission. If an employer breaches any of these, they may be required to pay union compensation to the affected employee totaling no less than their annual salary.

Article 24 of the Unions Laws dictates that employers cannot terminate union representatives without just cause. Termination notices must be in writing and explicitly explain the cause for termination. Union representatives or the union have one month from the termination notice receipt to initiate a reinstatement lawsuit. If the court decides in the union representative's favor, they have the right to receive all unpaid salaries and benefits owed them from the termination date to the court's decision date. If the union representative requests employment reinstatement within six days after the court's reinstatement decision, their salary and benefits must be paid during the continuance and/or extension of their duty as a union representative, even if the employer does not reinstate the union representative. These protective provisions also cover employees who are trade union managers and continue to work in the employer workplace. If either of the parties appeals to the first instance court's decision before the Regional Court of Appeals (*Bölge Adliye Mahkemesi*), then the decision of the Regional Court of Appeals will be final.

Article 118 of the Penal Code sentences those who prevent others from exercising their union rights or from resigning their union management duties to imprisonment for six months to two years. Union rights include membership or nonmembership to a union or participation in union activities. Those who block union activities through coercion, threat, or any other unlawful means will be imprisoned for one to three years.

9.6. Relocation of Work/Shutdown of Business

Collective bargaining agreements can be problematic for work relocation, as work relocation would require amending the agreement. The union and employer party to the agreements must negotiate the amendment and sign a protocol amendment to regulate work conditions.

If no collective bargaining agreement is in place, employers must consider whether work relocation is a substantial adverse change to each employee's working conditions. Substantial changes include situating the new workplace in an area that is difficult for employees to reach, or moving the workplace to a new city. All substantial adverse changes to the working conditions stipulated in the employment contract, workplace regulations, and workplace practices can be enacted only after obtaining the employees' written consent. The employer must notify their employees of the proposed change in writing, and they in turn must provide their consent in writing within six business days. If employees do not consent to the proposed change, they are not bound by said change.

The shutting down of the business does not invalidate a collective bargaining agreement; the agreement is in effect until the end of their term. If a workplace's employer changes, the new employer is bound by the collective bargaining agreement effective in that workplace. Following a shutdown, if the same employer or a new employer restarts the business in the same workplace, the collective bargaining agreement is in effect until its expiration.

Following the collective bargaining agreement's expiration, the provisions on employee working conditions remain in effect until a new collective bargaining agreement is executed.

9.7. Checklist of Dos and Do Nots

- Do not obstruct employees from exercising their union rights or participating in union activities.
- Employees cannot be terminated due to their membership or activities in a union.
- Cooperate with union members and unions. Enact their requests, so long as they are reasonable and not detrimental to the company or other employees.
- Negotiate the collective bargaining agreement's terms and benefits judiciously, as those may be in effect even after the agreement's expiration.

10. WORKING CONDITIONS: HOURS OF WORK AND PAYMENT OF WAGES BY STATUTE OR COLLECTIVE AGREEMENTS

10.1. Overview of Wage and Hours Law

While the Turkish Constitution asserts that employee salaries are a social right, the Labor Code oversees the regulations on employee salaries and working hours. Regulations such as the Minimum Salary Regulation and the Regulation on Principles of Overtime Work carry out the Labor Code's regulations on employee salaries and work hours.

The Labor Code defines salary as a cash amount paid to an employee by their employer or a third party, in return for their services. The base salary must be paid in cash only, and the law does not exclude any items from the definition of salary. Payments for annual leave, general and national holidays, and weekends are calculated in consideration of the base salary. The base salary and any benefits (such as the value of premiums, private insurances, company cars, bonuses, mobile phones, clothing) are utilized when calculating statutory seniority compensation and notice compensation.

An employer cannot ask an employee to work more than forty-five hours per week, generally divided equally for each day of a workweek.

The Labor Code regulates the distribution of working hours within a week and working hours within the weeks of a balancing period, which cannot exceed two months for regular employment contracts and four months for collective bargaining contracts. When discussing a balancing period, the employer and employee can agree to distribute the entirety of the working hours throughout the balancing period: for a balancing period of two weeks, the parties can agree that the employee will work more than forty-five hours in one week and less in the second week. In any case, the workday cannot exceed eleven hours of work and the average weekly working hours of the employee during the balancing period cannot exceed the regular weekly working hours.

10.2. Minimum Wage

Employers must deposit salaries in cash to the employees' bank accounts where there are at least five employees working with the employer in Turkey. Employers cannot discriminate against employees with the same or similar qualifications working under same or similar conditions in terms of their salaries. The Minimum Salary Fixing Board of the Ministry determines the mandatory minimum salary at the latest once every two years. The minimum monthly gross salary in 2022 for employees was determined as TRY 5,004 and its total cost to the employer was TRY 5,879.70. Within the Minimum Salary Fixing Board's decision on July 1, 2022, the minimum salary for employees became TRY 6,471.00 and its total cost to the employer became TRY 7,603.43. As per the decision, these amounts will be valid until December 31, 2022.

Salaries must be paid in Turkish Lira. The employer and the employee can agree to another currency provided that the foreign currency payment ban explained in section 12.1. does not apply for the relevant employment agreement. A salary denominated in foreign currency must be converted to Turkish Lira for the payment of the employee's taxes and social security premiums.

Failure to pay an employee their salary grants the employee the right to receive interest, to cease working, or to terminate employment based on just cause.

10.3. Overtime

Overtime is the time worked in addition to one's normal working hours, which is regulated as forty-five hours in one workweek. Work hours distribution based on a balancing period in which a workweek is longer than forty-five hours is not considered overtime.

Certain individuals cannot perform overtime work:

- employees younger than 18 years of age;
- employees who have provided a medical report that prohibits them from working overtime;
- employees who are pregnant, have recently given birth or are breastfeeding;
- part-time employees; and
- employees working in mines.

"Exceeding time" work is the time worked in excess of a workplace's working time hours which are determined to be less than the above threshold of forty-five working hours per week, but in any case up to forty-five working hours per week.

For overtime and exceeding time work, employers must obtain their employees' written consent at the beginning of the employment or when the need to work overtime arises. The written consent must be preserved in employee personnel files.

Employees can be requested to work overtime without prior consent in cases of national interest or urgency. What qualifies as urgency, such as mechanical problems, is determined on an individual basis.

The maximum annual overtime work is 270 hours. In their latest decisions, the Supreme Court of Appeals has determined whether an employee worked overtime by also reviewing if the employee has worked overtime more than 5.2 hours per week.

In calculating overtime hours and exceeding time, periods under thirty minutes are rounded up to thirty minutes and periods over thirty minutes are rounded up to sixty minutes.

Payment for an hour of overtime work equals 1.5 times the employee's regular hourly salary. Payment for an hour of exceeding work equals 1.25 times the employee's regular hourly salary.

An employee can request ninety minutes off for each overtime work hour and seventy-five minutes off for each exceeding time work hour instead of the abovementioned increased hourly salary. An employee can utilize their time off during work hours and without a salary subtraction within six months from acquiring the right to time off.

10.4. Meal and Rest Periods

Employers must provide employees with a break in the middle of their workday. The break must be proportionate to the hours worked:

- A fifteen-minute break for four or less working hours.
- A thirty-minute break for four to seven and a half working hours.
- A one-hour break for more than seven and a half working hours.

Break times are not taken into account in the calculation of working hours, i.e., they are not considered as working hours.

In theory, break times must be uninterrupted. Practically, the employer may, if stipulated in the employment agreement, divide break times into intervals due to climate, season, local traditions, or work characteristics. Employees working in the same workplace can be given breaks at the same or different times by their employers.

10.5. Deductions from Salary

Employers cannot deduct amounts from their employees' salaries unless so specified in the employment or collective bargaining agreement. Employers are prohibited to deduct an amount from an employee's salary as a disciplinary measure, save for the reasons specified in the employment or collective bargaining agreement.

The employer cannot set off an employee's salary in exchange for their receivables. Employers can only set off an employee's salary if the employee has given their prior written consent to do so, or the employee intentionally inflicted damages on the employer, as ruled by a final court decision. While there is no legal provision, scholars believe the amount subject to set off must not exceed one-fourth of the employee's monthly salary.

10.6. Garnishment

The transfer, pledging, and garnishment of employee salaries are restricted by Article 35 of the Labor Code and Article 410 of the Code of Obligations. Per these provisions, no more than one-fourth of an employee's monthly salary can be pledged, garnished, or transferred to a third party.

10.7. Exemptions to Wage and Hours Laws

While all employment relationships are subject to the legal provisions on salaries and working hours, additional regulations are applicable for certain employment relationships and working conditions. For instance, the Regulation on Indivisible Working Time establishes different working hour schedules for those working on vehicles traversing highways, railways, rivers, lakes, and seas; working in shifts; working at night; or working in mines. Also, specific working hours regime applies for the employees working in mines, shifts or at nights.

Following maternity leave, one of the employee parents can request to work part-time up until the end of the first month of that their child begins the mandatory education. The employer must accept post-maternity part-time working hours request, which cannot be ground for termination.

10.8. Child Labor

The Regulation on Child and Young Employees' Working Conditions defines young employees as those between 15 and 18 years old. Child employees are defined as those who are over the full age of 14 but under the full age of 15 and who have successfully completed compulsory primary education.

While the Labor Code states that children under 15 years old cannot be employed, those who have reached 14 years can be employed to perform light works that do not hinder their mental, physical, or moral development or their school attendance. Child employees under 14 years old can be employed to perform artistic, cultural, and advertising activities that do not hinder their mental, physical, or moral development or their school attendance. Employers must, for the employees who have not yet completed the full age of 14, execute a written employment agreement with the child employee and obtain the parental consent for each activity that the child employee will undertake.

Employers must take into account the health, safety, physical, mental, and psychological development, personal inclination and capability of child and young employees. Employers must ensure that a child employee's duties do not hinder their school attendance, professional education, or competence to regularly follow the classes or vocational training of which competence is recognized by the Ministry of National Education.

Young employees are prohibited from working underground, underwater and in industrial works in the nighttime. The Regulation on Occupational Health and Safety requires employers to obtain a medical report verifying a young employee's physical fitness to complete the assigned work, and their health must be monitored throughout the term of employment.

Young employees can work a maximum of eight hours a day and forty hours a week. Child employees who have successfully completed their compulsory primary education and do not continue their education further can work a maximum of seven hours a day and thirty-five hours a week. Child employees under 14 years of age and who are employed for artistic, cultural, and advertising activities can work a maximum of five hours a day and thirty hours a week. When a child employee completes 15 years of age, their maximum working hours can be increased to eight hours a day and forty hours a week. A child employee attending school can work a maximum of two hours a day and ten hours a week during the school year. When the school year is over, the above work-hours regime applies.

Child and young employees must be granted uninterrupted twenty days of annual paid leave.

10.9. Recordkeeping Requirements

10.9.1. Information That Must Be Maintained

The employer must keep a personnel file for each employee containing the employee's identity information and any legally required documents and records. The employer must comply with any requests from the relevant authorities to deliver hardcopy personnel files, such as during a Ministry-led audit. The employer must utilize the acquired employee information legitimately, in keeping with the principles of integrity, and without disclosing information considered confidential for the employee's just interest.

The statute of limitations for a majority of employee claims is five years. Accordingly, it is advised to retain personnel files for the duration of the employment relationship and for five years following the end of the employee's service. On the other hand, the Regulation on Occupational Health and Safety Services mandates that personnel's health files should be retained for a minimum of fifteen years following the end of employment.

10.9.2. Records That Must Be Retained

Various laws govern the documents requiring retention in personnel files. It is advised that the following particular documents be kept in personnel files:

- Copy of the employee's ID card.

- The work start notification filed with the SSI (*İşe Giriş Bildirgesi*).
- General health insurance registration notification filed with the SSI (*Genel Sağlık Sigortası Giriş Bildirgesi*).
- Notification of insurance filed with the SSI (*SGK Sigortalı Bildirim Belgesi*).
- Deployment notification following termination filed with the SSI (*Sigortalı İşten Ayrılış Bildirgesi*).
- Notification form relating to the employee's family status (*Aile Durum Bildirimi Formu*).
- Copy of job application.
- Copy of employment offer letter.
- Copy of the employment agreement.
- The employee's residence certificate (*İkametgah Belgesi*).
- For foreign national employees, copies of the work permit or work permit exemption certificate.
- The employee's pay stubs, preferably with the employee's signatures.
- The employee's educational information and records, including diplomas or certificates.
- Copies of the employee's CV and reference letters.
- The employee's health report concluded prior to employment.
- The employee's criminal record.
- Documents and/or forms about annual pay leave requests.
- Employee's annual pay leaves tracking document (*İzin Kayıt Belgesi*).
- For male employees, military service documentation.
- Delivery receipt record relating to the inventory delivered to the employee.
- For employees under 18 years of age, a copy of the written contract signed between the employer and the employee's parents or guardians.
- If there is no related provision in the employment agreement, the employee's written and signed consent to overtime and exceeding work.
- If there is no related provision in the employment agreement, the employee's written and signed consent to working on national and general holidays and weekly holidays.
- Documents delineating the administrative duties in the event of occupational accidents, and SSI occupational accidents notifications.
- Minutes of occupational accidents.
- For pregnant employees whose health condition so requires, a doctor's report ordering the increase of the statutory pre and post-birth leave periods.
- Documents evidencing the employee received the required Occupational Health and Safety Law training.
- Delivery receipt records showing the employee received the required occupational health and safety equipment.

- Copies of warning letters and/or defense requests delivered to the employee; the copies must be signed by both the employer and the employee.
- Copies of the employee's submitted defense letters.
- Warning letters and minutes for unexcused absences and tardiness.
- Following termination, the certificate of employment (*Çalışma Belgesi*) and a document signed by the employee evidencing that the certificate was delivered to the employee.
- Copy of the employee's resignation letter, signed by the employee.
- In especially employer directed terminations, a copy of the release letter signed by the employee.
- Minutes of the performance evaluation meetings.
- In case of collective termination, copies of the notifications filed with the relevant Regional Directorate and the respective labor union, and copies of the announcements made in the workplace about the collective termination.

10.9.3. Failure to Maintain Required Records

Failure to keep personnel files may result in administrative fines for the employer.

If an employer does not submit the personnel files or other information requested by the labor authorities for an investigation, thereby obstructing the investigation, the employer may face an administrative fine.

The amount of the aforementioned administrative fines varies each year.

10.10. Reductions in Compensation Caused by Economic Downturn

There is no provision in the Labor Code relating to reduction in compensation due to economic downturns. On the other hand, if the employee consents, in writing, such reduction can be made by the employer.

Employers can terminate employment agreements based on valid reasons due to financial and business necessities. In such a case, the employee is entitled to their entire termination entitlements, including notice compensation and statutory seniority compensation.

10.11. Checklist of Dos and Do Nots

- Working hours' practices must be in line with the relevant laws.
- Retain overtime work records.
- Pay employees at least the minimum monthly salary.
- Employ children and young employees in accordance with the relevant laws.
- Adhere to record maintenance requirements; be prepared for and comply with authorities' possible investigations and requests.
- Ensure that all information in personnel files is convenient and current.

11. OTHER WORKING CONDITIONS AND BENEFITS BY STATUTE, COLLECTIVE AGREEMENTS, OR COMPANY POLICY

11.1. Health and Other Insurances

The Social Security and General Health Insurance Law No. 5510 (the "Social Security Law") protects employees' social security rights. In particular, the Social Security Law protects individuals' social and general health insurances, stipulates the procedures and principles regarding the use and execution of these insurances, sets forth conditions for eligibility and the rights granted under these insurances, and covers the methods of financing and coverage for these insurances.

The Social Security Law governs short-term and long-term insurances. Short-term insurance covers health, maternity, occupational accidents, and diseases while long-term insurance covers old age, disability, and death.

The Social Security Law defines insurance holders as those who are:

- employed by one or more employer through an employment contract;
- the village and neighborhood headmen;
- individuals working independently who are: (i) income tax payers (through commercial or self-employment earnings); (ii) exempt from income tax, but registered with the relevant trader and artisan registries; (iii) shareholders who are also board of director members of joint stock companies, shareholders of other companies and all shareholders of maritime joint ventures, and active shareholders of a commandite company whose capital is divided into shares; and (iv) conducting agricultural activities;
- certain individuals working in public administrations.

Individuals employed through an employment agreement fall within the scope of the law, as per Article 4 of the Social Security Law. Employees must satisfy three conditions to be insurance holders:

(1) the employment relationship must be governed by an employment agreement;
(2) the agreed service must be conducted in the workplace; and
(3) the employee must not be categorized as an uninsured person as per Article 6 of the Social Security Law.

Individuals covered by short and long-term insurances are automatically holders of public insurance. The insurance rights and obligations cannot be removed, reduced, renounced, or transferred to a third party.

Workplaces and employees must be registered with the SSI before the employees start working there, as per Articles 11 and 8 of the Social Security Law, respectively.

11.2. Pension and Retirement Benefits

Statutory Pensions

Employers must register their employees with the SSI and pay their social security premiums, which are charged to the employees' monthly salaries. Premiums enable employees to enjoy both short and long-term insurance coverage, like health and retirement benefits. Social security premium payments are the responsibility of both the employee and the employer. Like social security premiums, income taxes are also accrued and deducted from employee salaries, and the employer then pays the employee's share directly to the government on their behalf:

SSI Premiums Type of Risk	*Employer's Share (%)*	*Employee's Share (%)*	*Total (%)*
Short-Term Risks (Occupational Accidents)	2	–	2
Long-Term Risks (Death, Old Age, Disability)	11	9	20
General Health Insurance	7.5	5	12.5
Contribution to Unemployment Insurance	2	1	3
Total	22.5	15	37.5

Short-term risk premiums depend on the severity of the employee's work. The total social security percent premium is 15% for the employee and 22.5% for the employer. If the employee's monthly salary exceeds TRY 37,530.00 for 2022, such capped amount will be taken into account when calculating the social security contributions for the employee.

Company Pension Schemes

Companies can establish company pension funds for their employees, but these are not subject to any regulation.

Private Pension System

Employees are automatically enrolled in private pension plans through an amendment to the Law on Private Pension Savings and Investment System No. 4632 (the "Law No. 4632"), which passed on October 7, 2001. The following employees qualify for automatic enrollment by their employers in private pension plans:

- who are under 45 years old;
- Turkish citizens or those who are no longer Turkish citizens but still enjoy the citizenship rights granted by the Turkish Citizenship Law No. 5901; and
- who work in the private or public sectors.

The Regulation on the Automatic Enrollment of Employees to a Pension System by Their Employers states that private-sector employees must be automatically enrolled in a private pension system according to the number of employees employed by their employer:

- Employers with 1,000 or more employees: January 1, 2017.
- Employers with 250–999 employees: April 1, 2017.
- Employers with 100–249 employees: July 1, 2017.
- Employers with 50–99 employees: January 1, 2018.
- Employers with 10–49 employees: July 1, 2018.
- Employers with 5–9 employees: January 1, 2019.

Employees over the age of 45 can be automatically enrolled in a private pension system, if they request so.

Employees must contribute 3% of their monthly salaries subject to their monthly social security premiums' calculation, which employers will automatically deduct from their salaries and pay to the private pension company. Employees can request a higher contribution rate. The contribution can be paid in foreign currency by Turkish citizens who are not legally resident in Turkey or those who are no longer Turkish citizens but still enjoy the citizenship rights granted by the Turkish Citizenship Law No. 5901.

Employees have two months to cancel their registration in the plan after receiving their notification of enrollment. After canceling their enrollment, employees will receive the contributions, plus any investment earnings paid to the private pension company within ten business days.

The state's contribution equals to 30% of the employee's contribution to the pension plan. If the employee does not cancel their registration in the plan, the state pays a one-off contribution of TRY 1,000.

The President of the Turkish Republic is authorized to reduce the state contribution rate down to 10%, with respect to the employee contributions paid in foreign currency. Currently, the state's contribution rate with respect to employee contributions paid in foreign currency is determined as 10%.

Per Law No. 4632, only companies established with the authorization of the Ministry of Treasury and Finance can provide private pension plans for the employers to enroll their employees in such plans.

Employers will be imposed an administrative fine for each violation of the automatic employee enrollment procedure.

Retirement and Pension Options

Within the scope of the statutory pension, employees can choose to receive their statutory pension retirement as salary or a lump-sum payment. The amount for each depends on the employee's circumstances, such as length of employment, total premium value, and the total number of days worked.

Private pension participants are eligible for retirement at 56 years old, as long as they have been enrolled in the system for a minimum of ten years. When a participant becomes eligible, they can choose to receive their accrued funds as a lump-sum payment or a monthly pension.

11.3. Vacation and Holiday Payments on Termination

To receive annual paid leave, an employee must have completed at least one year of service, including the probationary period. If the employee and employer agree, an employee can take their paid leave during the first year of employment. The one-year term includes any prior employment periods with the same employer.

Annual paid leave is contingent on the length of employment:

- one to five years of employment (including five years): fourteen working days;
- six (inclusive) to fourteen (inclusive) years of employment: twenty working days;

– fifteen and more years of employment: twenty-six working days.

Those performing underground work have the right to four additional paid leave days. Employers must allow employees to use their annual leave days without interruption, but if both parties agree, employees can take their leave in increments, as long as they take one interval of a minimum of ten days.

Unused annual paid leave is transferred to the next employment term and can be accrued. Following termination for whatever reason, the employee is entitled to receive the monetary equivalent of their untaken annual paid leave, calculated based on their last month's salary.

Employee absences from work due to illness or accident must be taken into account in terms of their length of service while determining their annual leave entitlement.

An employee terminated by their employer cannot have their annual leave days overlap with their notice period or any time off taken to procure another job.

11.4. Leaves of Absence

11.4.1. Personal Leave

Provisions for personal (unpaid) leave stipulated in employment or collective bargaining contracts are applicable, as the Labor Code does not regulate personal leave. If there are no agreements in place, the parties should mutually agree to personal leave conditions.

11.4.2. Medical or Sick Leave

Employers must grant an employee sick leave if they have submitted a medical report verifying their illness. If the recovery period for an illness or injury lasts over six weeks after the statutory notice period identified based on the employee's length of service, employers can terminate employment with just cause and without serving the notice period. For example, an employee who has worked for less than six months has a two weeks' notice period and if the employee is continuously absent due to illness for eight weeks (notice period plus six weeks of illness), the employer has the right to unilaterally terminate the employment. The employment field had continuing discussions on the necessity of employers obtaining the employees' defenses for termination of their employment agreements for just cause if the employees' illness-related absenteeism is six weeks longer than their notice period. Pursuant to the decision of the Supreme Court

General Assembly of Civil Chambers on the Unification of Decisions dated October 19, 2018 and No. 2017/9 E.–2018/10 K., employers are no longer required to obtain employees' defenses before terminating their employment agreements for just cause if employees were absent due to illness for an additional six weeks after the end of their notice period.

Employees who suffer illnesses or disabilities due to their lifestyles (disorganized living) or intention or alcoholism and are absent due to those reasons for three consecutive days or more than five business days a month can be terminated for just cause.

Sick leave is not contingent on a minimum employment period. Employers are not obligated to provide sick pay to employees during sick leave, unless employees receive fixed monthly salaries. Employees are entitled to compensation during this time through government disability programs, and the compensation is provided by the government starting from the third day of the illness, provided that the employee satisfies certain conditions. If employers pay their employees monthly fixed salaries, employers can deduct the government disability compensation employees receive starting from the third day of illness from their monthly salaries.

11.4.3. Bereavement Leave

If an employee loses their spouse, children, mother, father, or siblings, they are granted a mandatory three days' paid bereavement leave. Bereavement leave is not contingent on a minimum employment period.

11.4.4. Family Leave

An employee, who is the parent of a child unable to use at least 70% of their physical, mental, psychological, sensorial, or social functions or a child receiving treatment for a chronic disease, is entitled to ten days' paid leave annually. Only one of the parents can take family leave—either without interruption or in intervals—and they must provide a medical report confirming the child's disability or medical situation.

11.4.5. Pregnancy and Adoption Leave

Expectant women have the right to receive paid leave for any absences due to pregnancy examinations. Women have the right to take a total of sixteen weeks of maternity leave, divided as eight weeks prior to birth and eight weeks after birth. If the woman gives birth to twins or triplets, the eight-week period prior to birth will be extended to ten weeks. Maternity leave can be extended with a medical report taking into consideration the woman's health and nature of her work, if necessary. If a woman dies during or after birth, the father of the child can utilize her unused leave days.

Employees adopting a child can take three days of paid leave. If the child is under 3 years old, the employee is entitled to take eight weeks' leave. For married couples, only one spouse can benefit from this eight weeks' leave, which begins from the day the adopted child is delivered.

Female employees can also request an unpaid leave for up to six months following pregnancy leave of sixteen weeks (in case of twins or triplets, eighteen weeks). In case of adoption of a child under 3 years old, this unpaid leave will be granted to the adopting employee or one of the spouses. Employers must provide such unpaid leave, which will not be considered in terms of their length of service while determining the annual unpaid leave entitlement.

Expectant and breastfeeding employees cannot work more than seven and a half hours a day. If necessitated due to her health, and verified by a medical report, an employee must be assigned to duties suitable to her present condition.

Women who utilized their sixteen weeks of maternity leave can request an unpaid leave period equaling half of their weekly work hours. For women who gave birth to their first child, the unpaid leave period is 60 days; for women who gave birth to their second child, the unpaid leave period is 120 days; and for women who gave birth to their third or subsequent children, the unpaid leave period is 180 days per birth. Women who have given birth to multiples can take an additional 30 days. Women who have given birth to a disabled child can take 360 days of unpaid leave. The adoptive parent of a child under 3 years old can also request the unpaid leave periods described. During this period, the Labor Code provisions on breastfeeding will not be applicable. Employees can benefit from either the unpaid six months leave or the above unpaid leave periods.

One of the parents may request, in addition to the above leaves, from their employer to place them on a part-time schedule up until the end of the first month of that their child begins the mandatory education. Employers are obligated to fulfill this request, which cannot be deemed a valid reason for termination. If the employee's spouse is unemployed, the employee cannot request to work part-time. If an employee chooses to return to their full-time work schedule, they cannot utilize this right again for the same child. The employee must inform the employer, in writing and one month prior, of their intention to exercise their part-time work right or to return to full-time work. When the employee resumes full-time work, the employee hired to replace them for full-time work is automatically terminated. The employee, individually or with their spouse, who adopts a child below 3 years old is entitled to use this right starting from the actual delivery date of the adopted child.

Lastly, female employees are entitled to a total of ninety minutes of breastfeeding leave per day to feed their children below 1 year old. The time segments and the number of parts in which such leave will be used can be determined by the employee. The length of the breastfeeding leave is considered as part of the daily working hours.

11.4.6. Paternal Leave

Once his wife gives birth to their child, a male employee is entitled to five days of paid leave.

11.4.7. Injury at Work

The Social Security Law defines "occupational accident" as an insured individual, immediately or thereafter, becoming physically or mentally disabled:

- at the workplace;
- due to the employer's work which the employee had been carrying out on their own behalf and independently;
- due to work performed outside of the workplace, at the employer's request;
- during the use of a breastfeeding break; and
- while the employee comes or leaves the place where the work is performed by a vehicle provided by the employer.

The Social Security Law defines occupational disease as "temporary or permanent sickness, the state of physical or mental disability of the insurance holder as a result of the nature of work the employee engages with or the conditions of the work."

Following an occupational accident, employers must inform the relevant local police authority immediately and the SSI within three business days as of the accident.

The SSI and the Ministry can authorize their inspectors to investigate an accident in order to determine whether it is an occupational accident. If the inspectors determine it is not an occupational accident, or they determine that the information provided was inaccurate, those who reported the inaccurate facts or incited the accident/damage will bear the investigation expenses.

Following the identification of an occupational disease, the employer informs the SSI within three business days as of the date learning or being informed of the occupational disease. SSI's expenses and temporary incapacity payments are borne by the employer who did not submit an occupational disease notification form, or who deliberately misrepresented the relevant facts.

If the Health Committee of the SSI determines that the insured employee's earning power in their profession (*meslekte kazanma gücü*) is reduced by 10% due to an occupational accident or disease, the insured employee has the right to receive permanent incapacity income.

Employers who do not duly inform the SSI of a work accident within three business days of the accident's occurrence must pay for the insured employee's incapacity benefit up until the notification date.

Employers are responsible for SSI costs associated with their action to prolong the insured employee's treatment or for causing the insured to become disabled or exacerbating the degree of their disability by delaying or neglecting to perform their responsibilities.

The Ministry can inspect whether a workplace has correctly enforced the Occupational Health and Safety Law requirements. If the Ministry detects a life-threatening situation for the employees, all work must cease until the situation is remedied. The employer can object to the Ministry's decision within six business days of the receipt of such decision. The employer is obliged to continue paying their employees' salaries during the work cessation.

The employer will be fined for each safety breach, such as the failure to ensure safe workplace operation conditions, failure to enact measures to protect employee health, and failure to comply with any applicable legislation. The employer can face a penal or criminal liability if an injury, accident, or illness occurs in the workplace.

11.5. Checklist of Dos and Do Nots

- Duly register employees with the SSI.
- Grant employees applicable leaves and record these leaves and their details.
- Pay social security premiums on time and in full.
- Diligently record employee paid and unpaid leave days.
- If an accident occurs in the workplace, immediately notify the relevant authorities.

12. WORKERS' COMPENSATION

12.1. Overview

The Labor Code defines salary as a cash amount paid to an employee by their employer or a third party in return for their services. The base salary must be paid in cash only, and the law does not exclude any items from the definition of salary. Payments for annual leave, general and national holidays, and weekends are calculated based on the base salary. On the other hand, the base salary and any benefits (such as the value of premiums, private insurances, company cars, bonuses, mobile phones, clothing, etc.) are utilized when calculating statutory seniority compensation and notice compensation.

The Regulation on the Payment of Salary, Premium, Bonus and Other Benefits via Banks (the "Regulation") was amended by the Ministry through a regulation, which was published on May 21, 2016 and effective as of June 1, 2016. Following the changes introduced in the Regulation, if there are at least five employees, who are working within the scope of the Labor Code, or Maritime Labor Code No. 854, or the Press Code No. 5953, or out of the scope of the Press Code No. 5953 but within the scope of the Labor Code, employers are obliged to pay salaries in cash to the employee's bank account.

The Minimum Salary Fixing Board of the Ministry determines the mandatory minimum salary at the latest once every two years. The minimum monthly gross salary for employees until the end of 2022 is TRY 5,004 and its total cost to the employer is TRY 5,879.70.

Salaries must be paid in Turkish Lira; however, the employer and employee can agree to another currency provided that the foreign currency payment ban explained below does not apply for the relevant employment agreement. A salary denominated in foreign currency must be converted to Turkish Lira while paying the employee's taxes and social security premiums.

The amendments to Decree No. 32 Regarding the Protection of the Value of the Turkish Currency (the "Decree No. 32") published in the Official Gazette on September 13, 2018 introduced a ban on FX and FX-indexed payments for certain agreements between Turkish residents. These amendments in the Decree No. 32 require employers and employees to update their employment agreements by converting the remuneration (i.e., salary and benefits) to Turkish Lira, within thirty days as of September 13, 2018. The exemptions to these restrictions were later determined by the Ministry of Treasury and Finance. Accordingly, the following employment agreements can be executed as denominated in foreign currencies or indexed to foreign currencies:

- employment agreements where the employee is not a Turkish citizen;
- employment agreements where the employer is not a Turkish citizen;
- employment agreements executed by: (i) non-Turkish resident persons' Turkish branches, representative offices, and liaison offices and (ii) Turkish companies in which a non-Turkish resident person directly or indirectly holds 50% or more of the share capital or management control solely or jointly;
- employment agreements executed by the companies in free trade zones within the scope of their free trade zone activities;
- employment agreements performed abroad; and
- employment agreements of seamen.

Failure to pay an employee their salary grants the employee the right to receive interest, to cease working, or to terminate employment based on just cause.

Employers can determine to pay premiums (*ikramiye*) or bonuses (*prim*) to their employees under certain conditions and based on regular performance intervals. Pursuant to the Code of Obligations, employers must pay their employees' premiums regardless of whether they have been working for the employer on the pre-agreed date of premium payment. In other words, employers are required to pay their employees' premiums on a pro-rata basis if their employment terminates before the pre-agreed date thereof. Scholars also believe that this rule should also apply to bonus payments.

12.2. Checklist of Dos and Do Nots

- Pay salaries in cash.
- Comply with the foreign currency ban with respect to salary payments.
- If there are at least five employees, deposit salary payments to employees' bank accounts.
- Make no salary discrimination between employees possessing the same or similar qualifications and working in the same or similar conditions.
- Ensure employees are paid a salary equal to or above the mandatory minimum salary.
- Following employee termination, certify that the employee is paid their compensation accrued until the termination date, as well as any pro-rated premiums or bonuses the employee is entitled to.
- Repeatedly offering the same additional monetary benefits to an employee may constitute a vested right if the employee has a just expectation that the employer will provide said benefits indefinitely.

13. LEGAL FRAMEWORK FOR EMPLOYEE INVENTIONS

Under Law No. 6769 on Industrial Property Rights ("Industrial Property Law"), rights and title to a service invention shall belong to the employer if:

- created by the employee in the course of an employment relationship in a private entity or a public authority;
- made while performing, as obligated, the task to which he/she has been assigned;
- based to a great extent on the experience and work/activity of the private entity or public authority.

The provisions of the aforementioned Industrial Property Law regarding service inventions are mandatory and cannot be changed to the detriment of the employee. According to Article 115/6 of the Industrial Property Law, if the employer claims the full title of the service invention, the employee is entitled to request payment of "reasonable" remuneration. Such remuneration would be calculated based on the following criteria:

- economic value of the invention;
- the title and role of the employee; and
- the contribution of the employer to the creation of the invention.

If the employee demands payment of such remuneration, the employer cannot refrain from paying by claiming that the invention was not worth protecting. Article 115 of the Industrial Property Law regulates the general principles for employee remuneration while the Regulation on Employee Inventions, University Inventions and Inventions Created under State Funded Projects (the "Employee Inventions Regulation") entered into force on September 29, 2017, governs the specifics, such as the calculation methods, payment methods, and terms. In a partial or full ownership claim of the service invention, the employer is under a statutory obligation to remunerate the employee inventor adequately under an agreement or any other legal relationship. In a partial ownership claim, the employer's obligation to remunerate the relevant employee arises only when the employer uses the invention. The remuneration will be calculated based on the service invention's economic/commercial applicability, the employee's duties in the company and the company's contribution to the invention. In this scope, the Employee Inventions Regulation lays down the specific calculation methods for employee remuneration, the methods of payment, and the period.

Within the scope of the remuneration calculation, the Employee Inventions Regulation classifies service inventions into three groups, determined according to the employees' duties, the employer's contribution in the creation of the invention, and the conditions under which the employee created the service invention. The Employee Inventions Regulation states the employee remuneration for his/her service invention will be calculated by multiplying the profits obtained from the invention by the coefficients based on the invention's group and the ratio of the invention profits to the net minimum wage.

14. COMPANY'S OBLIGATION TO PROVIDE SAFE AND HEALTHY WORKPLACE

14.1. Overview of Safety Regulations

As the title implies, the Occupational Health and Safety Law oversees the occupational health and safety of all private and public works and workplaces, as well as their employers, representatives, and workers (including apprentices and interns) in every field. Every field has its own particular, additional regulations.

The Occupational Health and Safety Law's provisions have varying dates of effectivity:

(1) Articles 6 (occupational health and safety services) and 7 (occupational health and safety services support) entered into force/will enter into force:
   (a) Except for those working within the scope of the abolished Article 81 of the Labor Code on occupational health and safety services, on December 31, 2023 for public establishments and workplaces with less than fifty employees and falling under less hazardous workplace class.
   (b) On January 1, 2014 for hazardous or highly hazardous workplaces with less than fifty employees.
   (c) On December 30, 2012 for all other workplaces.
(2) Articles 9, 31, 33, 34, 35, 36, and 38, as well as provisional Articles 4, 5, 6, 7, and 8 entered into force on June 30, 2012.
(3) Other articles entered into force on December 30, 2012.

14.2. Requirements

Under the Occupational Health and Safety Law, employers must:

- Undertake every possible measure to protect their employees' health and safety, including providing information, training, organization, means, and equipment to prevent occupational risks, and make sure that the measures are adjusted in accordance with the changing conditions.

- Oversee and test that occupational health and safety measures are implemented, and ensure that any violations are eradicated or remedied.
- Perform a risk assessment, whether conducted by the employer or a third party.
- Consider employees' particular health and safety when assigning them tasks.
- Undertake measures to guarantee that employees who have not received the relevant training or instruction do not have access to hazardous areas.
- Appoint employees as occupational safety specialist, workplace doctor, and if there are ten or more employees in a highly hazardous workplace, appoint additional health staff. Employers must recruit a "Joint Health and Safety Unit" (*Ortak Sağlık ve Güvenlik Birimi*) to fulfill the occupational safety specialist, workplace doctor or additional health staff positions, if the employees are not sufficiently competent. If the employer possesses the necessary qualifications and documentation, the employer can offer those services, depending on the workforce number and workplace hazard category.
- Satisfy the requirements for means, space, and time to designate individuals or organizations to fulfill the workplace health and safety responsibilities.
- Guarantee the coordination and cooperation between all individuals and organizations appointed to provide workplace health and safety services.
- Exercise the health and safety measures that are in compliance with the legislation, and which are notified to the employer in writing by the designated individuals or organizations providing health and safety services.
- Immediately communicate to the designated individuals, external service providers, and employees any information received regarding situations that may affect, or are suspected to affect, employee health and safety. External or third-party employers and their employees working in the employer workplace must also be informed.
- Conduct health examinations for each employee during preassignments, employment, and work duty alterations following a reinstatement after an occupational accident, occupational illness, or another health-related event. During recruitment, request a health report from employees indicating that their health status allows them to fulfill their workplace tasks.
- Create an "Occupational Health and Safety Board" (*İş Sağlığı ve Güvenliği Kurulu*) for workplaces with fifty or more employees who are permanently employed for more than six months.
- Establish "Workplace Health and Safety Unit" (*İşyeri Sağlık ve Güvenlik Birimi*) at workplaces with certain criteria that need to employ a full-time workplace doctor and occupational safety specialist.

- Identify and assess potential states of emergency and take measures, including preparation of emergency plan and conducting drills, to minimize their effects. Also, the employer is responsible for employee evacuation from the workplace in an emergency situation.
- Provide occupational health and safety regulation training to every employee.
- Assign employee representatives, the numbers of which vary according to the total number of workplace employees. For instance, workplaces with two to fifty employees must designate one representative; workplaces with fifty-one and one hundred employees must designate two representatives.

Additional obligations may exist depending on the workplace's field of business.

14.3. Rights of Employees

All employees are entitled to workplace occupational health and safety, regardless of whether the workplace is private or public or of the total number of employees in the workplace.

Employees whose work performance poses a threat to their health or life can immediately terminate their employment and claim pecuniary and nonpecuniary damages.

If a grave and imminent danger arises in the workplace, the employees can request that the employer discern and remedy the danger. Employees can cease working until the danger is eradicated; employers must continue to pay salaries even if work is halted. Employees' contractual and legal rights are reserved.

If an employer does not heed the employee's requests for safety, the employee can terminate their employment. If employers are unable to prevent or resolve the grave and imminent danger, employees can exit the workplace and seek a safe place without requesting the employer to resolve the situation. Employers must respect their employees' safety rights.

If employees face a grave and imminent danger requiring their immediate action, and they cannot inform their managers of the danger, the employee is not liable for their immediate action unless he/she acted negligently or carelessly.

Employees returning to work after an occupational accident, occupational illness or other health reasons have the right to ask their employer to arrange a medical examination prior to recommencing their work.

Employees can provide their employer with occupational health and safety suggestions or concerns.

Article 20 of the Occupational Health and Safety Law provides employees the right to have an employee representative act on their behalf for occupational health and safety matters. The employee representative can participate in occupational health and safety-related studies, as well as make suggestions and request necessary remedial measures regarding occupational health and safety.

14.4. Rights of Employers

Employees must attend and apply the information learned in occupational health and safety trainings, as well as execute employer instructions related to occupational health and safety. Employees cannot compromise the health and safety of themselves or other employees who may be affected by their behavior or work. Under Article 25 of the Labor Code, employers have the right to terminate an employee for just cause if they do not follow the employer's occupational health and safety protocol, despite receiving employer warnings prior to termination.

Workplace machinery, tools, and equipment must be handled carefully, correctly, and in line with the workplace safety rules. Employees must not remove or alter the machinery or any of their safety mechanisms arbitrarily. Employees must use, maintain, and store the provided personal safety equipment correctly and safely. The employer can terminate an employee who, deliberately or by gross negligence, endangers the workplace safety or damages or misplaces the machines, equipment, or other workplace property and materials rented by the workplace to such an extent that the employee's thirty days' salary cannot pay for the damage suffered.

14.5. Specific Standards

The employer's specific requirements vary on the workplace's line of business and the work carried out there, as explained in section 14.2.

14.6. Injury or Accident at Work

Article 14 of the Occupational Health and Safety Law entrusts employers to maintain records, conduct the relevant investigations, and draw up reports on all workplace occupational accidents and illnesses. Employers must investigate and write reports for accidents which do not result in injury or death, but cause damage or has the potential to damage the workplace or their equipment, or harm employees.

Following an occupational accident, employers must inform the relevant local police authority immediately and the SSI within three business days as of the accident date.

Employers must inform the SSI of the occupational illnesses notified by health service providers or the workplace doctor, within three business days as of the date of such notification.

Workplace doctors or health service providers must notify the health service providers authorized by the SSI of the issues which they have, in the pre-diagnosis stage, classified as occupational illness.

Health service providers must also notify the SSI within at latest ten days of the occupational accidents they have been informed about. Also, the health service providers authorized by the SSI are required to notify the SSI within at latest ten days of the issues which they have identified as occupational illness.

Employees must immediately alert their employer or employee representative of any grave and serious danger to occupational health and safety in the workplace machinery, tools, equipment, workspace, or building. Employees who discover a problem with their current safety protocols must also immediately alert their employer or employee representative. If the relevant authorities identify any workplace occupational health and safety laws violations, employees must cooperate with their employer and employee representative to remedy the violations.

14.7. Workplace Violence

Workplace violence constitutes grounds for just cause termination under Article 25 of the Labor Code. Employers can terminate an employee due to just cause for assaulting a co-worker, within six business days of discovering the incident and the offender, provided that one year has not passed from the date the incident has occurred.

14.8. Fines and Penalties

Employers who fail to comply with their Occupational Health and Safety Law responsibilities may be subject to monetary fines, stop work, imprisonment, and prohibition from participating in public bids.

The employer will face administrative fines if the Occupational Health and Safety Law is violated, either per employee and/or per month during which the violation continues.

Workplace activities can be halted until a life-threatening workplace condition is remedied. These conditions may exist in the workplace building, "annexes of the workplace" (*işyerinin eklentileri*), working procedures, or the work equipment. Depending on the condition's specifics, such as the degree of hazard to employees, workplace activities can be halted partially or fully.

The relevant authorities can also halt workplace activities for workplaces that:

- are designated as highly hazardous and operate in the mining, metal, or construction sectors; or utilize hazardous chemicals in their work; or are under risk of a major industrial accident; or
- have not been subjected to a risk assessment.

If the employer or their representatives ignore the legal order to cease workplace activities, they face imprisonment for three to five years.

If a court decision determines that the employer of a mining workplace had fault in an employee's death due to an occupational accident, the employer will be prohibited from participating in public bids for two years. If the employing entity is a stock corporation (*sermaye şirketi*), individuals holding more than 50% of the entity's shares are also prohibited from participating in public bids.

The employer or their representatives can face criminal sanctions if they violate their occupational health and safety regulation responsibilities, resulting in injury or death of an employee in the workplace.

14.9. Checklist of Dos and Do Nots

- Ensure compliance with all relevant occupational health and safety laws and regulations.
- Undertake every possible measure to protect employees' health and safety, including providing information, training, organization, means, and equipment to prevent occupational risks.
- Oversee and test that occupational health and safety measures are in place and correctly executed.
- Promptly notify the SSI and local police authority of any occupational accidents and illnesses.
- Act appropriately and swiftly to remedy a grave and imminent danger, as requested by an employee; failure to do so grants the employee the right to terminate their employment agreement.

15. IMMIGRATION, SECONDMENT, AND FOREIGN ASSIGNMENT

15.1. Overview of Laws Controlling Immigration

The Law on Foreigners and International Protection No. 6458, entered into force on April 11, 2014, and the International Labor Force Law No. 6735, entered into force on August 13, 2016 and abolished the Law on Work Permits for Foreigners No. 4817, regulate immigration in Turkey. The Regulation on the Implementation of the Law on International Labor Force ("Regulation") has published in the Official Gazette dated February 2, 2022 and numbered 31738 and abolished the Regulation on the Implementation of the Law on Work Permits for Foreign Nationals ("Repealed Regulation"), which was in effect before February 2, 2022. With the Regulation, the determination, implementation and monitoring of policies regarding the international labor force, the procedures, principles, authorities and responsibilities related to work permits and work permit exemptions to be granted to foreign individuals, and rights and obligations in the field of the international labor force have been reregulated. It is regulated that the existing practices will continue to be applied until the necessary administrative and technical studies for certain new regulations are completed. Information on the completion of these studies will be announced on the Ministry's website.

Pursuant to the Law on Foreigners and International Protection Foreign, nationals who would like to extend their stay in Turkey beyond their visa or visa exemption period or more than ninety days must acquire a residence permit. The foreign national must submit their residence permit application to the Turkish embassy or consulate located in their home country or country of residence. While residence permit applications can be submitted through authorized intermediaries, they are, in practice, submitted directly to the immigration offices.

There are two steps to obtaining a residence permit. First, the foreign national must secure an appointment with the relevant immigration office, determined according to their residence address in Turkey. Second, the foreign national must attend their appointment at the immigration office in person and with their required documentation. Residence permit applications are generally processed and granted/denied within ninety days from the appointment date (i.e., from the application date).

Valid work permits or work permit exemption certificates function as residence permits; foreign nationals with valid work permits or work permit exemption certificates do not need to apply for a residence permit.

In principle, foreign nationals aiming to work in Turkey must obtain a work permit irrespective of the duration of their employment in Turkey.[3] To obtain a work permit, the foreign national must make an appointment with the Turkish embassy/consulate or visa/tourism agency located in their home country or country of residence and must attend their appointment in person with the required documentation. Authorized intermediaries can also execute a foreign national's work permit application. The International Labor Force Law defines authorized intermediaries as "institutions and organizations whose qualifications and tasks have been set out by the regulations and who have been authorized by the Ministry." Foreign nationals possessing a valid residence permit granting them a minimum stay of six months for a reason other than education can directly apply for a work permit to the Ministry in Turkey within the validity period, without the need for an appointment with the Turkish embassy/consulate or visa/tourism agency abroad (i.e., the foreign national's home country or country of residence).[4]

After applying to the Turkish embassy or consulate abroad, the foreign national's Turkish employer or their proxy must submit all required documentation to the Ministry within ten business days. The Ministry will not process applications submitted after the deadline.

In order to file work permit applications, the workplace, in which the foreign national will work, must be registered in the Ministry's electronic permit system (which can be accessed at the following link: https://ecalismaizni.ailevecalisma.gov.tr/#/eizin) by those who are responsible for the employer's social security notifications and can access this system through their electronic signature device (*e-imza*, in Turkish). Such responsible individuals can authorize third parties who can submit further work permit applications on behalf of the employer for the same workplace. Once the relevant registration is completed and the workplace's online account is created, the employer is able to submit work permit applications for other foreign nationals to be employed in this workplace with the existing registration. The employer can update the information of an already registered workplace at any time on this system. However, if a new workplace is established, this workplace must be registered in the electronic permit system in order to proceed with the work permit application for a foreign national who will work in the new workplace.

3. Foreign nationals intending to work in health and education services that require professional competence must fulfil a preliminary permit requirement prior to applying for a work permit.
4. The Turkish employer or their representative must submit the foreign national's online work permit application via the online account of the workplace in which the foreign national will work, to be created by visiting the Ministry's website (which can be accessed at the following link: https://ecalismaizni.ailevecalisma.gov.tr/#/eizin). The employer must submit all required documentation to the Ministry via the workplace's online account as soon as possible, but in any case within the validity period of the residence permit.

The International Labor Force Law states that the Ministry must process work permit applications within thirty days, but in practice, they take thirty to forty-five days, and even longer, depending on the Ministry's workload. Upon review, the Ministry notifies the relevant Turkish embassy or consulate, which grants the applicant a single-entry work visa at their discretion. While the Turkish embassy or consulate notifies the applicant when their visa can be collected, the applicant can also contact the Turkish embassy or consulate to coordinate the collection of their visa. The applicant must receive their work visa and enter Turkey within six months as of the work permit's validity date; if the applicant does not enter Turkey within the specified timeframe, the permit is invalidated.

After entering Turkey with the single-entry work visa, applicants must receive their work permit card prior to exiting the country. Work permit cards are mailed to the applicant's workplace after issuance, and grant the applicant the right to freely enter and exit Turkey during their validity.

All required application documents submitted to the Ministry must be in Turkish. Documents in foreign languages must be translated into Turkish and notarized by a Turkish notary public.

The Ministry applies the following criteria when processing work permit applications:

(a) The employers are required to employ a minimum of five Turkish nationals for every one foreign national (the "1:5 rule"). If the same employer has multiple workplaces registered in the social security system under its title, the 1:5 rule will be calculated based on the total number of Turkish nationals working in all of these workplaces.
In the businesses that fall within the category of Special Direct Foreign Investment, one foreign national, who qualifies as "key personnel" is exempt from the 1:5 rule both during the initial work permit application and also, in the work permit extension application. In this regard, as an example, in representative offices, branch offices or subsidiaries of foreign companies, which prove that the foreign company has another direct investment in another country (a country other than Turkey and the country where the foreign company has its headquarters), the individual, who has the authority to represent the representative office, branch office or subsidiary, is exempt from the 1:5 rule both during the initial work permit application and also, in the work permit extension application.
Any foreign national who will be hired in addition to the key personnel in the businesses that fall within the category of Special Direct Foreign Investment will be subject to the 1:5 rule; but in that case, the 1:5 rule will be calculated based on the total number of

Turkish nationals working in all workplaces of the employer in Turkey.

The representative of a liaison office of a foreign parent company, who has a valid power of attorney from the foreign parent company to officially represent the liaison office, is exempt from the 1:5 rule during the initial work permit application and also in the work permit extension application. Please see the below requirement for liaison offices, with respect to the foreign exchange they need to bring to Turkey from abroad, for work permit applications.

If the work permit application is filed for a foreign national, who will work for a company that is newly incorporated, and the submission is made in the first six months of the company's incorporation, the 1:5 rule will not be applicable to the respective foreign national during the initial work permit application. In any case, during the work permit extension application, the Ministry requires the employer to have hired five Turkish nationals, for the second six-month period of the respective foreign national's one-year work permit.

If any additional work permit applications are filed for other foreign nationals in the first six-month period of the company's incorporation, the 1:5 rule will apply to these additional foreign nationals, directly at the time of submitting the work permit applications.

The Ministry has the discretionary power to hold applicants exempt from the 1:5 rule, but such exemption is usually granted for a limited number of foreign national employees and a limited term. The Turkish employer is usually requested to justify the work permit application by explaining such as why such foreign national is, in particular, required for the job (i.e., why such job cannot be performed by a Turkish national) or what type of investments it will make to the Turkish economy once the respective foreign national is brought to work in Turkey.

(b) The employer's paid-in capital must be equal to a minimum of TRY 100,000, or their gross sales must be equal to a minimum of TRY 800,000, or the previous year's export amount must be equal to a minimum of USD 250,000. In case the employer is a liaison office, the liaison office must have brought at least USD 200,000 or foreign exchange that equals to such amount, from abroad to Turkey as part of the liaison office activities, in the last one-year period.

(c) Point (b) above does not apply to work permits of foreign nationals who have requested to be employed by *associations and foundations*, and points (a) and (b) are not applicable for the work permit applications of foreign nationals who aim to work for airlines agencies owned by foreign states, the education sector or in domestic services.

(d) The company shareholder applying for a work permit must have a minimum capital share of 20% at the company, and no less than TRY 40,000.
(e) The employer must pay the foreign national a monthly salary that matches with their skills and tasks. The employer must utilize the minimum salary amount requirement as of the work permit application date, as a base to set the monthly salary, which must additionally be a minimum of:
    (i) six and a half times the minimum monthly salary for pilots, top executives;
    (ii) four times the minimum monthly salary for branch or unit managers, architects, and engineers;
    (iii) three times the minimum monthly salary for positions that require mastery or specialization, physiotherapists, psychologists, teachers, musicians, and stage performers;
    (iv) two times the minimum monthly salary for massage or spa therapists, or acrobats and entertainers in tourism-animation organizations;
    (v) one and a half times the minimum monthly salary for work in professions other than those listed above (such as sales persons and marketing-export officers); and
    (vi) the minimum monthly salary for those who will work in domestic services.
(f) Points (a) and (b) are not applicable in the review of work permit applications in the field of purchasing goods and services through a *contract or tender by public bodies and institutions,* or under the conditions where a *bilateral or multilateral treaty* to which Turkey is a party contains a provision that allows such employment.
(g) Points (a) and (b) are not applicable in the review of work permit applications for positions that require *advanced technology expertise,* or if a Turkish expert with the same qualifications does not exist and the Ministry approves the foreign national's employment.
(h) In at least three-star and higher tourism establishments such as hotels, certified holiday villages, thermal hotels possessing massage parlors based on the required permission, facilities possessing Turkish bath-sauna-SPA parlor provided that they have contracts with certified tourism establishments, and gym centers where at least twenty Turkish nationals are employed, work permit applications for jobs requiring specialization and mastery (e.g., massage and spa therapist positions) will be assessed by the Ministry. The Ministry will not approve the applications of businesses falling outside of such scope.

(i) The 1:5 rule does not apply for foreign national positions requiring mastery and specialization in tourism-animation or entertainment companies that have hired a minimum of ten Turkish nationals.

Work permit applications can also ultimately be assessed on the Turkish employer's scope and objectives, as well as the foreign national applicant's professional experience and education.

The International Labor Force Law states that foreigners who graduated from a Turkish engineering or architecture program or from a university abroad recognized by the relevant foreign authorities and also the Turkish Council of Higher Education can work in Turkey as an engineer or architect for a certain project or on a temporary basis, based on a valid work permit. The following process is currently pursued for work permit applications of engineers, architects, and urban planners, until further changes.

First of all, a foreign diploma equivalent to a Turkish diploma in the field of engineering, architecture, or urban planning must be submitted to the Ministry.

Foreign nationals with degrees in engineering/architecture/urban planning from foreign universities may receive a preliminary one-year work permit; however, they cannot work in the fields of engineering/architecture/urban planning in Turkey during the validity period of such preliminary work permit. Prior to the expiration of the preliminary work permit, the foreign national must obtain an equivalency diploma from the Turkish Higher Education Institution to be able to apply for a work permit. In actuality, this may take the foreign national longer than one year to obtain the equivalency diploma, making the work permit application a challenging process.

Within one month of their arrival in Turkey, the foreign national who has a degree in engineering/architecture/urban planning should apply for temporary membership in their relevant professional chamber.

An employer can only hire a foreign national engineer/architect/urban planner if they have already hired a Turkish engineer/architect/urban planner.

The Ministry consults certain authorities, e.g., the Ministry of Public Works and Settlement and the Presidency of the Turkish Chamber of Engineers and Architect, regarding the issuance of work permits for engineers, architects, and urban planners.

Thus, in comparison to regular applications, the work permit applications for foreign nationals wishing to practice their careers as engineers, architects, and urban planners in Turkey take a longer time to be reviewed and approved.

Foreign nationals who will only manage and supervise engineering, architecture, or urban planning activities in Turkey, and not actively engage in these activities, and their employers need to sign an undertaking declaring as such. Accordingly, their work visa and work permit applications cannot indicate their position as "engineer/architect/urban planner."

Lastly, Turkish employers must register their foreign employees who have secured a work permit with the SSI (i) within at most thirty days from the work permit's validity date, if the work permit application is made within Turkey (i.e., as allowed for foreign nationals who have already been granted residence permits valid for at least six months—for any reason, except education) and (ii) within at most thirty days as of the date the foreign national enters Turkey with a single-entry work visa, if the work permit application is made from abroad (i.e., by visiting the Turkish embassy or consulate located in their home country or country of residence). Also, within twenty business days from their entrance into Turkey, the foreign employee must register address of residence in Turkey, with the Census Office (*Nüfus Müdürlüğü*).

15.2. Recruiting, Screening, and Hiring Process

Turkish law does not provide any additional or particular requirements on the recruiting, screening, or hiring of foreign nationals.

15.3. Obligation of Employer to Enforce Immigration Laws

It is illegal to employ a foreign national without a work permit or work permit exemption certificate.

In principle, all foreign nationals engaging in any kind of work-related activity must obtain work permits. Turkish employers are legally required to submit their foreign employee's work permit documentation, as well as file work permit renewals, to the relevant authorities. The only exception to this obligation is that it is stated otherwise in a bilateral or multilateral agreement to which Turkey is a party.

15.4. Fines and Penalties

Foreign nationals working in Turkey without a work permit will be subject to an administrative fine.

An employer or their representative employing a foreigner without a valid work permit will be subject to an administrative fine per undocumented employee. The employer or their representative is responsible for the foreigner's accommodation expenses, expenses to return to their home country, and any of their or their spouse and children's health expenses, if necessary.

The penalty amounts vary each year. Repeated violations will be fined double the penalty amounts. The relevant authority notifies the Ministry of Interior about foreigners without work permits for the deportation process.

15.5. Secondment/Foreign Assignment

Turkish immigration law does not regulate secondment or foreign assignment. Foreign nationals seconded or transferred to their employer's Turkish subsidiary must, therefore, secure a work permit, and be employed and paid salaries by the Turkish subsidiary. The procedures and processes delineated in sections 15.1.–15.4. above apply.

15.6. Checklist of Dos and Do Nots

– Foreign nationals who would like to extend their stay in Turkey beyond their visa or visa exemption period or more than ninety days must acquire a residence permit.
– Do not employ foreign nationals without obtaining a work permit for them. Doing so can result in the foreign national's deportation, as well as fines for both the foreign national and the employer or the employer's representative.
– Ensure that the Turkish employer submits all required documentation to the Ministry within ten business days after the foreign national submitted their work visa application to the relevant Turkish mission (i.e., Turkish embassy/consulate) and receives the necessary reference number from the Turkish embassy/consulate. For work permit application that is made within Turkey (i.e., as allowed for foreign nationals who have already been granted residence permits valid for at least six months—for any reason, except education), the submission must be made as soon as possible, but in any case within the validity period of the residence permit.
– Ensure that foreign nationals who have secured a work permit are promptly registered with the SSI and the Census Office and they collect their work permit card prior to exiting Turkey.
– When applying for work permit, take into account the Ministry's respective criteria for both the employer and foreign national.
– Heed the specific requirements to obtain work permits for foreign nationals to be employed as engineers, architects, and city planners in Turkey.

16. RESTRICTIVE COVENANTS AND PROTECTION OF TRADE SECRETS AND CONFIDENTIAL INFORMATION

16.1. Overview

Mainly the Code of Obligations regulates the restrictive covenants between the employer and employee, rather than the Labor Code.

Article 396 of the Code of Obligations regulates employee's confidentiality obligation. Accordingly, the employer has the right to terminate an employee for breaching their confidentiality obligation as a just cause.

The Code of Obligations also oversees non-competition and nonsolicitation agreements and penalty clauses deterring employees from misconduct towards their employer.

Certain employee actions, such as disclosing trade secrets, may trigger the Commercial Code's unfair competition principles.

16.2. The Law of Trade Secrets

The term "trade secret" is not defined under Turkish law. The Code of Obligations alludes to "confidential information" which scholars opine that it means any trade information or information regarding the employer's financial or personal conditions, including but not limited to their production, management, sales structure, and client portfolio.

The Supreme Court of Appeals dictates that general processes or preparations that are easily understandable or disclosed to third parties are not trade secrets.

16.3. Restrictive Covenants and Non-compete Agreements

Confidentiality

Employees have the obligation to exercise loyalty to their employer, which includes confidentiality. Employees must maintain confidentiality over all of the employer's business secrets, like technical expertise, client lists, supplier lists, prices; anything that is not publically available; and anything that is vital for the protection of the employer's business interests. As per Article 25 of the Labor Code, an employer can terminate an employee for violating their confidentiality obligation based on just cause.

The employee's confidentiality obligation can continue after the end of the employment relationship, if the employer has an interest in keeping the respective information confidential.

Non-competition

An employee is prohibited from performing activities that constitute competition with their employer's activities during the employment relationship, as a result of their duty of loyalty.

An employee and their employer can execute a written agreement setting forth that the employee is forbidden from engaging in any competitive activity against the employer or entering into any relationship with a competitor, even after the termination of employment. However, such restriction can apply only to an employee who knows production secrets, goodwill, or any information regarding the production process, dissemination of which would cause considerable harm to the employer.

A non-compete agreement must be reasonable in terms of the duration, region, and nature of the restricted work. Furthermore, without a legitimate reason, non-compete agreements cannot exceed two years.

The Code of Obligations provides that if a court finds the terms of a non-compete agreement to be excessive or unreasonable, the court can alter the terms to be in line with the law. The non-compete agreement must explicitly state its duration and the restricted territory. To increase the likelihood of enforceability, agreements should abstain from utilizing general area terms such as "Turkey," rather, they should designate specific areas, such as "Istanbul and Bursa" or "the Aegean region of Turkey."

While not statutorily required, employers should consider offering payment of consideration to employees during the non-compete period which can ensure enforceability of such restrictive covenant taking into account that the Supreme Court of Appeals tends to side with employees in most labor disputes.

Non-compete agreements can include penalties for the violation of the non-compete restrictions. Also, if reserved and where necessary, the employer can request cessation of the violation through court-mandated injunctions or similar orders.

16.4. Checklist of Dos and Do Nots

- Prepare restrictive covenants cautiously, as they may not be enforceable against employees.
- Take the proper measures to prevent employees from accessing material trade secrets or knowledge, if not necessary.

17. PROTECTION OF WHISTLEBLOWING CLAIMS

17.1. Overview

While Turkish law does not provide any regulations or protection for whistleblowers, companies can create internal policies on this issue.

17.2. Checklist of Dos and Do Nots

- Take any and all possible measures to protect and prevent retaliation against whistleblowers such as keeping their identity confidential.
- If the issue reported by the whistleblower is serious and can lead to termination of employees, initiate an investigation within six business days of discovery, and complete the investigation promptly.

18. PROHIBITION OF DISCRIMINATION IN THE WORKPLACE

18.1. Overview of Antidiscrimination Laws

Article 10 of the Turkish Constitution, Article 5 of the Labor Code, and the Law on the Turkish Institution of Human Rights and Equality govern the principles of equality. Section 3.2. offers a detailed summary of the Law on the Turkish Institution of Human Rights and Equality.

Article 10 of the Turkish Constitution states that all human beings are equal under the law, without any distinction, including but not limited to language, race, color, sex, or political, philosophical, and religious beliefs.

Article 5 of the Labor Code similarly prohibits the discrimination of an individual engaging in an employment relationship based on but not limited to language, race, color, sex, disability, or political, philosophical, and religious beliefs.

Providing employees with different salaries, bonuses, and social benefits like daily food allowances, transportation allowances, and clothing, based on the employees' qualifications, positions, working conditions, and seniority, does not violate the prohibition of discrimination. However, employers who differently treat employees who possess similar qualifications and work in similar or same conditions must be able to justify the different treatment with vital reasons. Discrimination between part-time and full-time employees and indefinite-term and definite-term employees without justifiable reasons is unlawful under the Labor Code. Employers cannot discriminate against employees based on gender or pregnancy/maternity, unless they have reasons to do so based on the nature of the work or reasons related to biological differences between males and females. Employers cannot provide different remuneration to employees performing similar jobs or work of equal value.

If a court determines that an employer discriminated against an employee, they can grant the employee discrimination compensation up to four times the employee's monthly salary and any benefits previously denied.

18.2. Age Discrimination

While Article 5 of the Labor Code does not explicitly refer to age as a condition requiring protection against discrimination, the provision covers "similar reasons," which is likely to include age. Depending on the specific circumstances, courts can prohibit ageism. As per the Law on the Turkish Institution of Human Rights and Equality, if it is required to employ a person at a certain age due to the nature of work, then discrimination allegation due to age will not be acceptable, provided that such criteria are necessary and proportionate for the work.

18.3. Race Discrimination

The Turkish Constitution states that all individuals are equal before the law, without distinction of race. Article 5 of the Labor Code specifically regulates the prohibition of racism in employment relationships. Article 3 of the Law on the Turkish Institution of Human Rights and Equality also condemns and prohibits race discrimination.

18.4. Sex Discrimination/Sexual Harassment

Employers cannot discriminate based on gender. Certain circumstances, i.e., the nature of a job or reasons related to biological differences between males and females, may allow employers to distinguish between genders in filling a position. Employers cannot discriminate against an employee in the conclusion, conditions, execution, and termination of their employment contract due to the employee's gender or due to pregnancy/maternity.

Employers must pay the same salary to employees of different genders performing similar jobs or work of equal value. Employers cannot argue for the payment of lower salaries for employees who receive special protective provisions due to their gender.

Article 417 of the Code of Obligations states the employer must ensure the protection of their employees against sexual harassment. Employers must protect and respect the employee's personality rights, demonstrate concern for their health, and ensure that decent moral standards are maintained. Employers must ensure that employees are not sexually and psychologically harassed, and that any harassment victim does not suffer additional negative consequences.

Employees can terminate their employment if an employer sexually harasses them under Article 24 of the Labor Code. The same article allows employees to terminate their employment if another employee or third party sexually harasses them and the employer did not take appropriate measures to halt or prevent the harassment from reoccurring, despite being aware of the behavior.

Article 3 of the Law on the Turkish Institution of Human Rights and Equality prohibits gender discrimination but stipulates that allegations of gender discrimination are invalid if the employer is required, due to the nature of the job, to employ a specific gender.

18.5. Handicap and Disability Discrimination

Article 5 of the Labor Code prohibits discrimination based on an employee's disability. Similarly, Article 3 of the Law on the Turkish Institution of Human Rights and Equality prohibits discrimination based on a person's health conditions.

Article 30 of the Labor Code stipulates that 3% of all employees, in a private-sector workplace employing over fifty employees, must be disabled employees.

Article 14 of the Law on Disabled Persons No. 5378 states that employers cannot discriminate against an employee in any aspect, including recruiting, working conditions and periods, career advancement, and occupational health and safety concerns.

18.6. National Origin Discrimination

Article 3 of the Law on the Turkish Institution of Human Rights and Equality prohibits discrimination based on an individual's origin and/or ethnicity.

18.7. Religious Discrimination

Article 3 of the Law on the Turkish Institution of Human Rights and Equality and Article 5 of the Labor Code prohibit discrimination based on an individual's religion or personal ideology.

18.8. Military Status Discrimination

Military status-based discrimination is not prohibited under the Turkish law. In practice, employers prefer hiring candidates that have completed their military service in order to avoid replacing an employee when they are called to serve.

18.9. Pregnancy Discrimination

Employers cannot discriminate based on an employee's pregnancy. Certain circumstances, such as a job being unsuitable for the health of a pregnant individual may warrant employers to recruit candidates or assign employees who are not pregnant.

Employers cannot discriminate against an employee in the conclusion, conditions, execution, and termination of their employment contract due to the employee's pregnancy.

18.10. Marital Status Discrimination

While Article 5 of the Labor Code does not explicitly refer to marital status as a condition requiring protection against discrimination, the provision covers "similar reasons," which is likely to include marital status. The Law on the Turkish Institution of Human Rights and Equality explicitly prohibits discrimination based on marital status. Depending on the specific circumstances, courts can prohibit employers from marital status discrimination.

18.11. Sexual Orientation Discrimination

While Article 5 of the Labor Code does not explicitly refer to sexual orientation as a condition requiring protection against discrimination, the provision covers "similar reasons," which is likely to include sexual orientation. Depending on the specific circumstances, courts can prohibit employers from sexual orientation discrimination.

18.12. Retaliation

Turkish law does not regulate retaliation, although the general provisions of tort may be applicable on a case-by-case basis.

18.13. Constructive Discharge

An employee who resigned due to reasons ascribable to their employer can request statutory seniority compensation. Other employee compensation claims are reserved, such as mobbing compensation.

If a court finds an employer guilty of discrimination, it may award the employee discrimination compensation up to four times the employee's monthly salary and any relevant benefits previously denied. The burden of proof to establish the veracity and evidence of the employer's discriminatory behavior lies with the employee.

Article 25 of the Unions Law declares that employers cannot discriminate against employees who are or are not union members, or who are different union members in terms of their working conditions and terminations. Employers who violate this article may pay union compensation equaling no less than the discriminated employee's annual salary. An employee cannot concurrently claim union compensation and unjust termination compensation.

In reinstatement lawsuits, the burden of proof for a termination's legality lies with the employer, unless and until the terminated employee claims the termination reason is different from the employer's claim. In union and certain discrimination compensation claims as applicable, the burden of proof lies with the employee to ascertain he/she was terminated due to union-related activities and not for the reason claimed by the employer. If an employer conducted large-scale terminations in which the majority of those terminated were union members, and did not hire any union members as part of the replacement personnel, the terminated employees may have a valid argument and evidence for compensation claims.

18.14. Checklist of Dos and Do Nots

– Follow the discrimination regulations.

- Take proper measures to protect the discriminated individuals and to discipline those that discriminate.
- Be prudent always when it comes to employee treatment, and particularly more if a collective bargaining agreement is in place.

19. SMOKING IN THE WORKPLACE

19.1. Overview

The Law on the Prevention and Control of the Damages of Tobacco Products No. 4207 (the "Law on Tobacco Products") prohibits the consumption of tobacco products in any closed areas of private and public workplaces. The Law on Tobacco Products provides certain exemptions, allowing the establishment of tobacco consumption areas in:

- Nursing homes, prisons, and hospitals for mental and neurological disorders.
- The decks of marine vessels transporting passengers between cities or countries.
- Assigned smoking hotel rooms.
- Assigned areas in venues conducting outdoor sports, art, culture, and leisure activities.

Individuals under 18 years old are prohibited from entering tobacco consumption areas.

Article 5 of the Law on Tobacco Products foresees administrative fines for offenders. Therefore, employees must abide by the Law on Tobacco Products' provisions and their employer's internal policies.

Certain regulations, including the Regulation on the Protection of Employees from the Dangers of Explosive Areas, the Regulation on Occupational Health and Safety in Mining Workplaces, the Regulation on Health and Safety Measures in Works Involving Asbestos, and the Regulation on Health and Safety Measures in Works Involving Carcinogenic and Mutagen Materials, also prohibit tobacco product consumptions.

Article 25 of the Labor Code stipulates that an employer can terminate an employee for just cause for endangering the safety of the work, whether willfully or through gross negligence. For example, an employee working in an explosives factory who smokes in the production area endangers the safety of the work can be terminated for just cause.

19.2. Checklist of Dos and Do Nots

- Establish smoking regulations within the workplace.
- Notify employees that smoking in the workplace is strictly forbidden and monitor the consumption of tobacco products in the workplace.
- Establish a smoking area outside of the work premises for employees.

20. USE OF DRUGS AND ALCOHOL IN THE WORKPLACE

20.1. Overview

The Occupational Health and Safety Law prohibits employees from attending work under the influence of alcohol or drugs and consuming alcohol or drugs in the workplace. Employers can terminate offending employees for just cause. The employer can determine appropriate times and conditions for alcohol consumption in areas that are "annexes of the workplace" (*işyerinin eklentileri*).

The prohibition of alcohol consumption is not applicable to certain employees:

- who are working in workplaces that produce alcoholic beverages, and due to the nature of their work, are responsible for auditing their production;
- who are working in workplaces where alcoholic beverages are consumed or sold, and due to the nature of their work, must consume alcoholic beverages;
- who, due to the nature of their work, must consume alcoholic beverages with their clients.

The Supreme Court of Appeals states that if the employee consumes alcohol outside the workplace, but the alcohol amount does not affect their behavior and work, this should not be considered just cause for termination.

20.2. Checklist of Dos and Do Nots

- Prohibit alcohol and drug consumption in the workplace to avoid accidents and injuries. Monitor that employees comply with the alcohol and drug consumption regulations.

21. AIDS, HIV, SARS, AND BLOOD-BORNE PATHOGENS

21.1. Overview

Under Article 25 of the Labor Code, employers can terminate employees based on just cause for health reasons, including AIDS, HIV, SARS, or blood-borne pathogens.

Employees can be terminated:

- For just cause, immediately and without notice, if they contracted an illness or suffered an injury due to their own deliberate actions and lifestyle choices, resulting in their absence from work for three successive business days or for more than five business days in a month.
- For just cause, immediately and without notice, if the Health Committee determined the employee's illness is incurable and their employment in the workplace is risky.
- If they contracted an illness or health condition not due to their deliberate actions or lifestyle choices, suffered an accident, became pregnant, or gave birth, and are absent from work for more than six weeks over the employee's notice period. In cases of pregnancy and birth, the employee's six-week period begins after their maternity leave ends. Suspended employees do not receive salaries during their suspension.
- For just cause, immediately and without notice, if they suffer from AIDS, HIV, SARS, or blood-borne pathogens, although these can be problematic terminations due to discrimination claims. In a recent case where an employee was suspended and forced to resign after their employer discovered that he/she was HIV positive, the Turkish Constitutional Court ruled that the employee had their material and moral presence and private life violated. The Turkish Constitutional Court based its decision on the fact that the relevant courts failed to examine the employee's claim, that he/she was unfairly forced to resign, and whether the employer genuinely looked for alternative positions for the employee in their workplace.

21.2. Checklist of Dos and Do Nots

- Offer employees regular health checks.
- Monitor employees' health if it becomes necessary to utilize the right of termination for health reasons, in order to exercise the right in a timely manner and protect the other employees and the workplace.

22. DRESS AND GROOMING REQUIREMENTS

22.1. Overview

Under their right to issue directives and manage the workplaces, employers can establish dress and grooming policies for their workplaces. Dress and grooming requirements can be determined and imposed in employment contracts, workplace regulations, and/or employer directives.

Employer directives must comply with the law: they cannot request employees to work without the necessary protective clothing relevant to their position. Employees must abide by the employer's legal instructions.

Employees who do not abide by their employer's directives or policies are in breach of the employment contract. Offenders may be required to pay compensation, as per the Code of Obligations, or suffer disciplinary sanctions, as per their employment contract or workplace regulation. Article 25 of the Labor Code allows employers to terminate employees who repeatedly and deliberately refuse to comply with their duties, despite receiving warnings for just cause.

22.2. Checklist of Dos and Do Nots

- Issue workplace regulations or policies on dress and grooming requirements.
- Review the workplace's occupational health and safety regulations to determine the protective clothing, which the employees are required to wear.
- Provide employees with and ensure that they wear suitable protective clothing.

23. PRIVACY, TECHNOLOGY, AND TRANSFER OF PERSONAL DATA

23.1. Privacy Rights of Employees

Individuals have the right to protect their personal data. It is prohibited to process or export abroad personal data, unless permitted under a particular law or with the data subject's explicit consent. Refer to section 3.6. for information on the Law on Personal Data.

Currently, cross-border transfer of personal data is allowed only based on explicit consent as a rule. However, cross-border transfer is possible without consent, if the data controller has a legal basis for the transfer (e.g., prevailing legitimate interest, which might apply for employers) and if one of the following conditions exists:

- the target country has an adequate level of protection as determined by the Turkish Personal Data Protection Board (no country has been announced as safe yet);
- both parties of the transfer sign a written commitment (based on Turkish Personal Data Protection Authority's template) and obtain Turkish Personal Data Protection Board's approval; or
- the group implements Binding Corporate Rules and obtain Turkish Personal Data Protection Board's approval.

If none of the foregoing conditions exists, explicit consent of the employee might be the only available legal basis for cross-border transfers.

Article 75 of the Labor Code obliges employers to utilize employee data in accordance with the applicable laws and the principle of good faith and maintain all data confidential if the employee possesses a justifiable interest to maintain their data confidential.

Article 419 of the Code of Obligations states that employers can only utilize employee data to determine whether the employee is suitable for the work or to the extent necessary for the performance of the employment contract.

Employers can access and examine all company equipment provided to employees for business purposes, such as laptops and mobile phones. Employers should notify employees of their right to access company equipment in their employment contracts and/or workplace regulations and ensure that employees sign each page of the aforementioned documents.

The Turkish Constitutional Court decided that an employer had legitimate interest to examine its employees' work e-mail accounts to discern whether they were being utilized for personal purposes and in line with the workplace policies in a case where the employees had been appropriately informed about this practice when they reviewed and signed each page of their workplace policies. Thus, employers should state in their workplace policies or employment agreements that employers can review their employees' business phones and computers, as well as business e-mail correspondence and phone calls, at any time. Employees should review and sign each page of the workplace policies and employment agreement documents.

Under Article 135 of the Penal Code, the illegal recording of personal data can be penalized by imprisonment for one to three years, and pursuant to Article 136 of the Penal Code, the illegal transfer, publication, and collection of personal data can be penalized by imprisonment of two to four years.

23.2. Checklist of Dos and Do Nots

- Notify employees of data processing activities relating to personal and/or sensitive data, informing employees what data will be collected, for what purpose, where it will be sent, that they have the right to demand their data be deleted, and that their data will be adequately protected.
- Inform employees in writing that their business phones and computers, as well as work e-mail correspondence and phone calls, can be reviewed at any time. Ensure employees review and sign each page of the relevant workplace policies and employment agreement documents.

24. WORKPLACE INVESTIGATIONS FOR COMPLAINTS OF DISCRIMINATION, HARASSMENT, FRAUD, THEFT, AND WHISTLEBLOWING

24.1. Overview

In Turkish law, there is no legal guidance on establishment of internal investigations, regulations, disciplinary procedures, and disciplinary committees. The Code of Obligations foresees employers' obligation to protect their employees' personal rights and dignity. Employers should implement the proper regulations and sanctions concerning fraud, theft, harassment, and whistleblowing.

Employers can establish internal discipline regulations for workplace investigations to ensure a cooperative, peaceful, and safe workplace. Case law determines that the general principles of law apply to internal discipline regulations:

- disciplinary penalties can only be enforced if they have a legal basis;
- employers must inform employees of the internal disciplinary regulations prior to enforcing any penalties;
- disciplinary penalties must be proportionate to the breach;
- the provisions must be equally applicable to all employees;
- the employer must respect its employees' right to self-defense; and
- following an internal investigation, the employer cannot retaliate against an unsubstantiated complaint or whistleblowing if the complaint did not have the intention to willfully harm the alleged offender.

24.2. Checklist of Dos and Do Nots

- Provide employees with internal discipline regulations written in Turkish and ensure employees sign copies of the regulations.

- Do not deduct any amounts from salaries, save for the reasons stipulated in employment or collective bargaining contracts.
- In an investigation, include the relevant employees in the process and offer them a fair chance to defend themselves.
- Document every aspect of investigations, disciplinary breaches, and penalties enacted.

25. AFFIRMATIVE ACTION/NONDISCRIMINATION REQUIREMENTS

25.1. Overview

Certain employees have the statutory right to special protection and the modification of their working conditions, such as:

- pregnant and breastfeeding employees (they cannot perform certain tasks, must be transferred to another position if their current position poses a danger to their condition, and must be permitted breaks to breast-feed or pump);
- young employees (they must be given shortened working hours and no overtime or night work);
- employees supervising children or individuals requiring special care and assistance (they can request shortened working hours and cannot be required to go on business trips without first granting their explicit consent); and
- disabled individuals.

Additional antidiscrimination provisions protect the above-listed employees:

- Under Article 30 of the Labor Code, private-sector workplaces with fifty or more employees must comply with a disabled employee quota equaling 3% of the total number of employees. If the employer has more than one workplace within the same city, the total number of employees in those workplaces is used as the base for calculation. Employees can request the aid of the Turkey Labor Institution (*Türkiye İş Kurumu-İŞKUR*) to employ disabled employees. Employers failing to comply with this quota will be subject to an administrative fine for each disabled employee it should have hired and for each month the violation is not rectified. The penalty amount varies each year.
- Employers cannot discriminate based on gender. Certain circumstances, i.e., the nature of a job or biological differences between males and females, may warrant employers to distinguish between genders in filling a position. Employers cannot pay an employee doing the same or similar

work as an employee of the opposite gender a lower salary because of their gender. Women cannot be required to work underground or underwater. If a woman terminates her employment within one year following her marriage, she is entitled to statutory seniority compensation.

- Expectant and breastfeeding employees cannot work more than seven and a half hours a day. If necessitated due to her health and verified by a medical report, an employee must be assigned to duties suitable to her present condition. If no suitable duties exist, the employee is entitled to unpaid leave if requested. Employers cannot require expectant employees to work nightshifts from the moment a health report verifies their pregnancy up until one year after their child's birth.
- The Labor Code defines young employees as those between 15 and 18 years old. Employers are prohibited from hiring individuals under 15 years old (refer to section 10.8. for the guidelines on child employees). Young employees cannot work underground, underwater, and in industrial sites/works in the nighttime. Young employees cannot work more than eight hours a day and forty hours a week. Employers must obtain a health report prior to hiring a young employee.
- Article 25 of the Unions Laws states that employers cannot discriminate against employees who are or are not union members, or who are different union members in terms of their working conditions and terminations. Employers failing to abide by these provisions may be ruled to pay compensation equivalent to no less than the relevant employee's yearly salary.

25.2. Checklist of Dos and Do Nots

- Identify the special employee groups in the workplace; recognize and ensure that their needs and conditions are met.
- Comply with the nondiscrimination policies related to each special employee group.

26. RESOLUTION OF LABOR, DISCRIMINATION, AND EMPLOYMENT DISPUTES: LITIGATION, ARBITRATION, MEDIATION, AND CONCILIATION

26.1. Internal Dispute Resolution Process

Parties to an employment contract can agree to internally resolve disputes and sign a settlement agreement. The Labor Code does not regulate internal dispute resolutions.

An internal committee cannot review a termination decision once the decision has been communicated to the addressee, this being the employer or employee. If an employer intends to terminate an employee, they must refer the termination decision to the relevant internal committee prior to informing the employee.

26.2. Arbitrary Mediation and Conciliation

The Law on Mediation in Civil Disputes No. 6325 (the "Mediation Law") allows for arbitrary mediation in civil disputes wherein the parties have the right to act based on their own discretions and dispose of the right. As such, a mediator can hear employment-related disputes. An employer or employee can apply to a mediator, continue, finalize, or cease mediation. The parties involved can agree to mediation prior to or during a lawsuit. Mediation is a discretionary dispute resolution mechanism and is uncommon in employment-related disputes.

The mediator or mediators are chosen by the parties unless another procedure is determined. The parties can attend the mediation meetings by themselves or through their legal representatives or lawyers. The persons who have the expertise and may contribute to the resolution of the dispute can be kept available at the mediation meetings.

Confidentiality is essential in mediation. If the mediator or parties involved violate confidentiality and damage the counterparty's rights, they may be imprisoned for up to six months.

The parties will enter a settlement agreement at the end of mediation. In case of a settlement, the parties cannot initiate lawsuit with regard to the subject of the settlement. If a party does not comply with the terms of the settlement agreement, the counterparty can apply to a court for the agreement's execution.

The parties can request the courts to issue an enforceability annotation for the settlement agreement. If the settlement agreement is signed by the parties, their lawyers and the mediator, the settlement agreement is deemed an agreement having the force of judgment.

The Unions Law offers official mediation as a resolution mechanism for collective disputes. Parties can request a mediator appointment from the Directorate of the Labor and Work Institution (*Çalışma ve İş Kurumu İl Müdürlüğü*) (the "City Directorate") if:

- one of the parties does not attend the negotiation meeting;
- one of the parties refuses to begin negotiation;
- one of the parties refuses to continue negotiation;

- one of the parties renders a report concerning nonagreement to the terms in a collective bargaining agreement;
- the negotiation concludes without reaching an agreement.

If one of the parties does not request a mediator appointment from the City Directorate within six business days as of any of the above occurring, the union's authority to negotiate a collective bargaining agreement is rescinded.

The City Directorate must appoint a mediator within six business days as of receiving a request. The Regulation on Mediation and Arbitration in Collective Bargaining Agreements vests a selection committee with the authority to prepare a list of authorized mediators and publish the list in the Official Gazette. The City Directorate must meet with one of the parties to decide on a mediator from this list. If no parties meet with the City Directorate, they can nominate a mediator from the authorized list at their sole discretion.

The mediator can settle with the parties within fifteen days from receipt of the mediation notification. If the parties want to extend this period for another six business days, they must inform the City Directorate.

If the parties are unable to reach an agreement until the end of the mediator's authority to settle the dispute, the mediator has three business days to prepare a report with advice and suggestions to resolve the collective disputes and submit the report to the City Directorate. The City Directorate must inform the parties of this report within three business days from receipt of the report.

At the end of the mediation period, the union in question can go on strike within sixty days from receipt of the mediator's report or apply to the High Board of Arbitration. Refer to section 26.3. for further details on the arbitration process for collective disputes.

26.3. Arbitration

The Labor Code allows for employers and employees to resolve their disputes through arbitration only if: (i) the dispute is a reinstatement claim; and (ii) within two weeks as of the date of the nonagreement before the mediator.

According to the Supreme Court of Appeals, an arbitration clause agreed to in an employment agreement prior to the occurrence of a dispute is void. The parties are not bound by pre-agreed arbitration clauses in both collective bargaining and employment agreements.

The Unions Laws provide that parties may only resort to arbitration to resolve collective disputes at the end of the mediation process explained in section 26.2. The High Board of Arbitration resolves collective disputes. The High Board of Arbitration is composed of the senior heads of the Supreme Court of Appeals' departments and consists of:

- A member selected by the Council of Ministers from a pool of individuals possessing knowledge and experience in economics, social policy, management, or labor law; that does not have any ties to worker or employer organizations; exercises no function in any political party organs; and is not affiliated with the ministries.
- A member selected by the Council of Higher Education from the teaching staff of a universities' labor law and social security law departments.
- The General Manager of Labor of the Turkish Republic Ministry of Labor and Social Security.
- Two members selected by the employees' confederation with the highest number of members.
- Two members selected by the employers' confederation with the highest number of members, one of whom is from public employers.

The relevant union votes on whether to strike; if the union decides not to strike, it can apply to the High Board of Arbitration within six business days after finalizing the decision. In disputes concerning workplaces or activities in which calling a strike is prohibited, one of the parties can apply to the High Arbitration Board within six business days from the receipt of the mediator report, as detailed in section 26.2. If a mediation period ends without reaching an agreement, one of the parties can apply to the High Arbitration Board after the applicable period. If none of these measures are taken, the union rescinds its authority to negotiate a collective bargaining agreement.

The High Board of Arbitration's decision is final and has the same effect and force as the collective bargaining agreement.

In collective disputes, the parties can resort to special arbitration at any stage. Collective bargaining agreements without arbitration clauses are subject to the Code of Civil Proceedings No. 6100. If the parties of a collective dispute agreed, in writing, to resort to special arbitration, the provisions on mediation, strike and lockout, and statutory arbitration are not applicable.

The special arbitration decision has the same effect and force as a collective bargaining agreement.

26.4. Mandatory Mediation and Litigation

Starting from January 1, 2018, it is a must to apply to mediation before filing a lawsuit concerning employee or employer receivables and compensation (statutory seniority compensation, notice compensation, overtime pay, etc.), and reinstatement claims. The mandatory mediation requirement is, however, not applicable to pecuniary and nonpecuniary compensation lawsuits arising out of workplace accidents or occupational diseases and their related recourse lawsuits. Lawsuits that are filed without their parties first undergoing mediation will be dismissed on procedural grounds due to the lack of cause of action.

The mediator must conclude the mediation within three weeks. In case the circumstances so require, this term can be extended for a maximum of one week.

If the parties reach a consensus at the end of the mediation, they cannot file a lawsuit regarding the issues agreed to in the mediation meetings. If, on the other hand, the parties cannot reach a consensus at the end of the mediation, the plaintiff can file a lawsuit before the courts.

Labor Courts, which are specialized labor courts established under the Law on the Labor Courts No. 7036, are competent to resolve employment-related disputes. The Labor Court resolves conflicts between employers and employees arising from employment agreements and any labor law-related claims, including the Labor Code, the Social Security Law, and the Unions Law.

The competent labor court is the one located in the district of the employer's headquarters or workplace. The labor courts located at where (i) the work is fulfilled, (ii) the workplace accident or the harm occurred or (iii) the injured employee is located are also competent. The parties to the employment agreement cannot determine which labor court hears their dispute.

Labor courts tend to side with employees. They expect strong documentary evidence from employers, an expectation loosely enforced for employees.

26.5. Fines, Penalties, and Damages

Failure to comply with labor regulations results in administrative fines, civil remedies, and criminal sanctions.

Civil remedies applicable for employers include:

- cancellation of an employer transaction or action, such as termination of the employment agreement;
- payment of compensation to the employee for items listed under the Labor Code, such as notice compensation and bad faith compensation; and
- employment reinstatement.

Civil remedies applicable to employees are the termination of the employment agreement and the payment of compensation to the employer as per the Code of Obligations' general principles.

Failure to comply with the Labor Code, the Social Security Law, and the Occupational Health and Safety Law results in administrative fines for the employer. Violations include failing to enact the adequate measures to protect employees' health, failing to pay social security premiums and failing to notify authorities of particular events or conditions within the appropriate time.

Failure to comply with labor norms results in criminal sanctions for employers. Under the Penal Code, employers who discriminate against their employees or inhibit employees from exercising union rights may be punished with short-term imprisonment, which may be converted into judicial fines. The most severe criminal sanctions apply to employers who have caused or failed to prevent employee injury or death in the workplace.

26.6. Checklist of Dos and Do Nots

- Remember that labor courts are overwhelmingly employee-friendly.
- Prepare for litigation by recording and maintaining all applicable documentary evidence.

27. EMPLOYER RECORDKEEPING, DATA PROTECTION, AND EMPLOYEE ACCESS TO PERSONNEL FILES AND RECORDS

27.1. Overview

The information for section 27 can be reviewed in sections 3.6., 3.9., 10.9., and 23.

27.2. Personnel Files

Refer to sections 3.6., 3.9., 10.9., and 23.

27.3. Confidentiality Rules

Refer to sections 3.6., 3.9., 10.9., and 23.

27.4. Employee Access

Refer to sections 3.6., 3.9., 10.9., and 23.

28. REQUIRED NOTICES AND POSTINGS

28.1. Overview

Article 109 of the Labor Code regulates employment-related notifications. Notifications must be executed in writing and bear the addressee's signature. If the addressee refuses to accept the written notification, at least two individuals that witnessed the addressee's refusal must write their names, the date, and their signature on the notification.

An employee's termination for valid reasons must be served in writing, save for cases where the employee refuses to sign the termination, as explained above. Serving the notification in writing is a matter of validity. Conversely, the written termination notice for termination on just cause is a matter of proof, not validity; as such, the notice can take any form. The termination notice is recommended to be issued in clear written form.

Employers must inform employees in writing of any substantial changes to their working conditions if the changes may be to the employees' detriment. Employers must obtain their employees' written consent for substantial working condition changes within six business days as of the employees' receipt of the notification consisting of the proposed changes.

28.2. Checklist of Dos and Do Nots

- Deliver all notifications to employees in writing and obtain their wet signatures to verify delivery. If employees refuse to accept the written notification, document the situation with minutes of failure to accept notification. At least two individuals that witnessed the addressee's refusal must write their names, the date, and their signature on the notification.
- Serve a termination notice for terminations for valid reasons in writing; any other mediums invalidate the termination notice.
- Serve a termination notice for terminations for just cause in writing as evidence.
- Notify employees of any substantial changes to their working conditions in writing and obtain the employees' written and wet-signed consent.

www.ingramcontent.com/pod-product-compliance
Ingram Content Group UK Ltd.
Pitfield, Milton Keynes, MK11 3LW, UK
UKHW020148290926
15471UKWH00004B/757

9 789403 503363